KING ALFRED'S COLLEGE
WINCHESTER

Library: 01962 827306

KT-466-066

To be returned on or before the day
marked below, subject to recall

THE OBERON GLOSSARY OF THEATRICAL TERMS

Over 1300 technical, backstage, acting, musical, dance and showbusiness terms in common usage.

by Colin Winslow

Oberon Books
London · England

First published in 1991 by Oberon Books Limited
8 Richardson Mews, London W1P 5DF England
Telephone: 071-383 5569

Typeset by O'Reilly Clark, London
Printed by Latimer Trend & Co. Ltd., Plymouth
Text typeset in Garamond ITC

ISBN 1 870 259 26 2

Oberon Books Limited

8 Richardson Mews, London W1P 5DF England
Telephone: 071-383 5569

Publishing Director: James Hogan
Managing Director: Charles Glanville
Associate Editor: Nicholas Dromgoole MA (Oxon), FIChor

For Robin

EDITOR'S NOTE

I am indebted to the many people who have helped with the compilation of this book. They are far too numerous to mention individually, so I hope they will forgive me if I confine myself to expressing my gratitude to *all* who have helped – my friends and colleagues who have patiently answered my questions, but especially my students at Northbrook College and Mountview Theatre School who have enthusiastically offered their help and for whom this book was originally created.

Colin Winslow
London

OBERON BOOKS LIMITED

8 Richardson Mews, London W1P 5DF England

Tel: 071-383 5569   Fax: Phone main number

Title

Absolute Hell
Rodney Ackland £5.50

Apart from George
Nick Ward £4.95

Brand
Ibsen, translated and adapted by
Robert David MacDonald £6.50

The Cabinet Minister
Sir Arthur Wing Pinero £4.95

Court in the Act!
Marcel Hennequin and Pierre Veber, translated by
Robert Cogo-Fawcett and Braham Murray £4.95

Enrico Four
Pirandello, translated by Robert David MacDonald £4.95

Faust
Goethe, translated by Robert David MacDonald £6.50

Mary Stuart/Joan of Arc
Schiller, translated by Robert David MacDonald £6.50

Mean Tears/In the Blue
Peter Gill (two plays) £4.95

No Orchids for Miss Blandish
Robert David MacDonald from the novel by
James Hadley Chase £4.95

Northern Star/Heavenly Bodies/Pentecost
Stewart Parker (three plays) £6.50

Oedipus the King/Oedipus at Colonus
Sophocles, translated by Christopher Stace £4.95

Old King Cole
Ken Campbell £4.95

The Pied Piper
Adrian Mitchell £4.95

Sidewind
Ray Brennan £4.95 (Autumn 1991)

The Strangeness of Others
Nick Ward £4.95

Susan's Breasts/Naked Robots/The Paranormalist
Jonathan Gems (three plays) £6.95

Travels with my Aunt
Graham Greene, adapted by Giles Havergal £4.95
(Autumn 1991)

Webster/Summit Conference/Chinchilla
Robert David MacDonald (three plays) £6.95

FOREWORD

"Oh, Lord! He will dissolve my mystery."
(Sheridan, *The Rivals, Act V, sc iii*)

Anyone who has ever had to call a plumber, let alone try to fathom a computer handbook, will be fatally familiar with the bewilderment of the outsider exposed to the shop-talk of professions other than his or her own. Indeed, there seem to be certain professions based, and depending, entirely on such mystification for their very continuance: accountancy, the law – "We have here a perfectly clear case of gibberish and double replevin, with manutectation *in partibus et utero*, have we not?" "Quite so, m'lud." – medicine, the building trade – "You'll need all your back-grulsing repanded . . . (hissing intake of breath) . . . Cost y'a few bob, that will . . ." – and how many of us really understand our insurance policies, or every word of a French menu – "Mouclade d'Aunis au pineau, embeurré de pétoncles Jules Verne sur son cataplasme de palourdes aux neiges d'antan"? I ask you!

Outlandish almost extra-planetary jargons, bandied between colleagues in a seemingly effortless desperanto, reduce the observer to an impotence only to be cured by reaching deeper into the pocket, or, failing that, by ignominious retreat into the murkier, more hopeless regions of D.I.Y.

"Art and mystery" was, perhaps still is, a formula employed in indentures for apprenticeship to a trade: the old trade-guilds were called "mysteries", and it is tempting, though alas inaccurate, to trace an etymological connection with the old mystery plays which, performed in cycles by the guilds, trundled through mediaeval cities on the wagons that were for centuries the actors' homes, in days before such books as the one you are holding became necessary. "Mystery" is still at the base of professional collegiality, and for two reasons: to stop penetration of the trade by non-union labour, and to ensure that terms used solely in the trade shall have an unambiguous exactness, referring to one article, function or operation only, with no overtones or undertones of everyday usage, a meaning as pure as the sound of a tuning fork. Ambiguity may be the lifeblood of imaginative literature, but it can play havoc when one wants things done in a hurry.

The theatre has its jargon like any other profession: beleaguered as its members often feel themselves to be, its slang often proliferates faster and more exotically than in more secure avocations – where else would going to lunch have been spoken of as "rounding out one's career" (30's USA), or a weekly receipt of salary be known as here under *Ghost?* A third function of shop-talk surfaces here, the need for embattled minorities to protect themselves from the vulgar gaze of "civilians".

And now here comes the author of this treacherous tome, with the authority, knowledge and experience of over a quarter of a century's work as a theatrical designer, technician and teacher, and blows the gaff on the whole business. The age of innocence is dead: No longer will we disingenuously think of a flat as somewhere to live, or of an apron as something by whose strings we were once tied to our mothers. Who would smoke hemp as here defined? Floods, floats, Frenchmen, teasers, travellers, tormentors, take on meanings no reasonable man could predict; in an anarchic overturning of the natural order, flies become places things are hauled up into, rather than the reverse; "things fall apart, the centre cannot hold" – as the senses reel, even "size" ceases to be a dimensional concept. Colin Winslow has much to answer for, though it may be as well that a phrase, such as I once heard from an impeccably liberal but temporarily irate Technical Director: "Strike the blacks and kill those bloody workers", will, as Freud said of asparagus, no longer be open to misinterpretation by the uninitiated. That said, each copy of this invaluable volume should carry a warning: "Caution: this book could seriously jeopardize your amateur status."

Robert David MacDonald
Citizens Theatre
Glasgow

GLOSSARY
OF
THEATRICAL TERMS

A

Above   Situated UPSTAGE of another object or performer.

Absurd theatre   See THEATRE OF THE ABSURD.

A.B.T.T.   Association of British Theatre Technicians. Not a trade union, but a society for the exchange of information. Talks on technical subjects and BACKSTAGE visits are frequently arranged.

Accompanist   A versatile musician (usually a pianist) who supports a solo singer, musician or dancer. At auditions accompanists may be required to transpose music, play at widely varying speeds or even by ear. They play an important part in a performer's success. Distinguished artists sometimes employ their own accompanist.

Accordionist   A once popular performer in VARIETY.

Ack-ack   See ACTING AREA LANTERN.

Acoustics   The sound quality in a specific space.

Acoustic shell   A structure specially built to reflect sound waves and improve ACOUSTICS. Frequently a temporary arrangement of built pieces used on stage for concerts and other musical events.

Acrobat   A performer of physical feats, once a popular VARIETY act and still an essential ingredient of the CIRCUS.

Act   To perform a role in a play.

One of several sections into which a play is divided, often with an INTERVAL between. Acts are often subdivided into SCENES. Plays now generally consist of two or three Acts, but four or five Acts were more popular until the early years of the twentieth century.

An item in a VARIETY show or CIRCUS.

Actable   Possible to be acted convincingly.

Act drop   Painted CLOTH or curtain sometimes lowered instead of HOUSE TABS at the end of each Act.

Acting area   Those parts of the stage on which any action or performance takes place.

Acting area lantern   (Abbr. ACK-ACK) A wide beam, non-focusable lantern, now generally obsolete.

Acting A.S.M.   An A.S.M. who may act small roles in addition to performing STAGE MANAGEMENT duties.

Acting edition   A published PLAYSCRIPT intended for use in the preparation of a production rather than for general reading. It usually contains practical STAGE DIRECTIONS and notes of PROPS and effects. (See FRENCH'S ACTING EDITION).

Action   Physical movement on stage. (See also BLOCK).

Narrative thrust of a dramatic performance.

Actor   One who performs in a play.

Actor manager   A theatre manager who also performs leading roles in productions he presents. Famous actor managers of the past include David Garrick (1770-1779), Edmund Kean (1787-1833) and Sir Henry Irving (1838-1905).

Actors' Church   St. Paul's Church, Covent Garden. Many famous actors have commemorative plaques around the walls.

Actors' Church Union   An interdenominational Christian organisation for actors.

Actors' Studio   An actors' training centre founded in New York by Lee Strasberg in 1947. Training was based upon the techniques of Constantin Stanislavski (1863-1938) and became known as THE METHOD, hence METHOD ACTING.

Adagio act   A VARIETY act popular in the early years of the twentieth century, in which a male and a female dancer perform a ballroom style dance routine in evening dress.

Ad lib   An unrehearsed line of dialogue occasionally inserted for comic effect, or to cover a lapse of memory or a technical error. Not generally encouraged.

Advance bar   A SPOT BAR hung across an AUDITORIUM, near the PROSCENIUM ARCH.

Agent   One who finds theatrical employment for artists and negotiates contracts on a commission basis. (Usually 10%). To cynics: One who resents the fact that an artist takes 90% of his earnings! (See LITERARY AGENT).

Agit-prop   (Abbr. of Agitation and Propaganda) Partisan political theatre usually associated with the hard left.

Aisle   Space between seating units for public access to seats. Theatre licensing regulations determine the number of aisles, and require that they are completely unobstructed during a performance.

Aldwych farce   Type of FARCE performed at the Aldwych Theatre in London during the 1930's and early 40's. Plays such as *Rookery Nook* by Ben Travers were popular, many starring Ralph Lynn and Robertson Hare.

Alienation   Dramatic technique developed by Bertolt Brecht (1898-1956) to compel audiences to consider the ideas presented in his plays without over-emotional involvement. (e.g. lettered signs, songs and deliberate anachronisms).

Amateur theatre Any performance in which participants are not professionals. Amateur performers have certain advantages – fewer financial pressures, lengthy rehearsal periods, the availability of a large pool of actors and guaranteed enthusiasm.

American Equity The American theatrical trade union. (cf. EQUITY).

Amphitheatre An ARENA stage surrounded by stepped banks of seating.

Alternative name for a tier of seating in an old style AUDITORIUM, such as The Royal Opera House, Covent Garden.

Angel One who invests money in a production for a share of the profits. Large numbers of angels will often contribute relatively small amounts, spreading the financial risk.

Apache dance Dance for a male and a female dancer, in which the man appears to ill-treat his partner using stylised acrobatic techniques suggestive of a Parisian thug.

Apron Extension of the stage projecting into the AUDITORIUM.

Arabesque In dance, a posture with one leg stretched backwards parallel to the floor, body bent forwards from the hips.

Arena A performance area entirely surrounded by the audience.

Aria Solo song in an OPERA, OPERETTA or oratorio.

Aristotle (384-322 BC.) Greek philosopher whose writings form the basis of dramatic theory. (See UNITIES, POETICS).

Artiste Performer, usually in VARIETY.

Artistic director A DIRECTOR with overall responsibility for the artistic policy of a theatre or theatre company.

Arts Council for Great Britain Organisation formed to encourage development of the Arts, distributing Treasury funds in the form of grants to theatres and other bodies. In recent years its function has become increasingly proscribed by central government with disappointing results for many companies which have had their grants cut back or withdrawn.

Asbestos curtain (American) SAFETY CURTAIN.

Aside A line of dialogue addressed directly to the audience and assumed to be unheard by other characters on stage.

A.S.M. Assistant Stage Manager. The lowest position in the STAGE MANAGEMENT hierarchy, but an essential one. Duties are innumerable, but include finding and making PROPS, assistance at rehearsals and performances, cleaning and tidying BACKSTAGE areas, running errands and making tea. (cf. ACTING A.S.M.)

Audition Test of a performer's suitability for a specific role or as a member of a COMPANY. Physical appearance, quality of voice and other individual characteristics are taken into account.

Audition speech A SPEECH, usually taken from a play, to demonstrate an actor's ability at an AUDITION.

Auditorium That part of the theatre occupied by the audience during a performance.

Auntie (or AUNTIE BEEB) The British Broadcasting Corporation. (B.B.C.).

Author The PLAYWRIGHT.

Autochange Device for changing the coloured GELS in a LANTERN by remote control.

Avant-garde New, experimental work.

B

Baby spot   Small SPOTLIGHT, less than 500 watts.

Backcloth   See CLOTH.

Backdrop   See CLOTH.

Backing   Piece of scenery positioned behind any opening in a SET such as a doorway or window, to hide the OFFSTAGE area.

Financial support for a production.

Vocal or instrumental accompaniment.

Backlight   Light arranged to strike the performers from behind for extra definition and sculptural effect.

Back projection   The process of projecting an image on to a screen or CYCLORAMA from behind. Useful for avoiding the shadows cast by performers or scenery by front projection.

Back projection screen   Screen made from translucent material specially developed to give a clear image when projected on from behind.

Backstage   The areas of the theatre surrounding the stage and not generally open to the public.

Backstage drama/comedy/musical   Genre of play or MUSICAL COMEDY in which actors play actors appearing in a show. It offers the opportunity for the inclusion of scenes from the SHOW WITHIN A SHOW. *Chorus Line* was a recent WEST END and BROADWAY example.

Balancing act   Any ACT in which performers demonstrate skill in controlling balance, either by balancing the whole body upon a piece of equipment, or by balancing objects such as clubs, hoops or balls upon various parts of the body, often with a partner or partners. Popular in VARIETY and the CIRCUS. (See PLATE SPINNING ACT).

Ballet   Dance work, complete in itself or included in another stage work. Ballet ranges from full length nineteenth century classical ballets (*The Sleeping Beauty*), romantic ballet (*Giselle*), to modern abstract works.

Ballet blanc   (French) White ballet. The classical ballet in which female dancers wear the traditional white ballet skirts, either long or short.

Ballet master/mistress   One responsible for training and rehearsing dancers in their roles, and giving classes.

Balletomane   An enthusiastic ballet-goer.

Ballyhoo   To swing FOLLOW SPOTS about energetically for spectacular effect.

Band   The theatre orchestra.

Band room   Musicians' changing room, usually beneath the stage.

Banjo   (or BANJO TRACK) Continuous double TAB TRACK with a banjo-shaped loop at each end, enabling a painted CLOTH or curtain, wider than the normal width of the stage to be drawn across to bring extra sections into view. Rarely used nowadays.

Bar   See BARREL.

Bar bells   FRONT OF HOUSE warnings to the audience that the performance is about to begin, given by means of an electric bell operated from the PROMPT CORNER.

Barker   One who draws patrons to a fairground attraction by shouting.

Barn doors   Adjustable metal shields added to the front of a LANTERN to trim the sides of the beam.

Barnstormers   Travelling players who used to perform in barns and similar locations. Nowadays "barnstorming" is a derogatory term for crude acting.

Barrack   To disrupt a performance by shouting from the audience.

Barre Horizontal wooden rail fixed to the wall of a dance studio, or free-standing, used to support dancers while practising.

Barrel (or BAR) Horizontal metal pipe, suspended from the FLIES, to which scenery or lighting equipment may be attached when FLOWN.

Barrel sling Short length of chain with a spring hook at one end, used for suspending one BARREL beneath another.

Bastard prompt A PROMPT CORNER situated STAGE RIGHT instead of the more usual STAGE LEFT.

Baton Slim wand used by conductors to beat time.

Batten Length of timber (usually 3" x 1") used for constructing and reinforcing scenery.

Long length of timber attached to the top and/or bottom of a CLOTH to support it and ensure that it hangs flat.

LIGHTING BATTEN: Group of LANTERNS suspended in a row above the stage. (See also COMPARTMENT BATTEN).

Batten pocket Deep open-ended hem sewn into the bottom of a CLOTH into which a BATTEN can be inserted to hold the cloth flat.

Beamlight Type of LANTERN without a lens, producing a parallel beam by means of a parabolic reflector.

Bedroom farce FARCE exploiting the humour of sexual impropriety.

Beeb (The) British Broadcasting Corporation (B.B.C.). (See AUNTIE).

Beginners Performers who appear at the beginning of a performance or ACT. (See HALF).

Below Situated DOWNSTAGE of another object or performer.

Benefit (performance) Special performance where the

proceeds are given to a deserving performer or worthy cause.

Berliner ensemble Theatre company founded in East Berlin by Bertolt Brecht (1898-1956) in the late 1940's, mainly devoted to his own plays and adaptations. The techniques of acting and staging he developed had far reaching effects. His plays, strongly political, frequently contained songs and music, such as *Mother Courage* and *The Threepenny Opera*. (See ALIENATION).

Bifocal (spot) SPOTLIGHT producing a hard or soft edged beam by means of an additional pair of shutters.

Big top A large CIRCUS tent. (American) The CIRCUS.

Billing The display of a performer's name on advertising material. When a performer is given "billing" his name is guaranteed to appear on any posters advertising the show, and often his contract will precisely specify size, position and other details. (See TOP OF THE BILL).

Billy block An obsolete movable wooden pulley, still occasionally used in FLYING SYSTEMS.

Biog (Abbr. for BIOGRAPHY) Short biographical details of a performer included in the PROGRAMME.

Birdie A mini PARCAN LANTERN. So named in punning reference to the golfing expression – a "birdie" being "one below par".

Black comedy Genre in which humour is extracted from tragic, cruel or bizarre situations and events.

Black light See U.V.

Blackout Extinguishing all stage lights to obtain total blackness, often used to heighten the dramatic effect at the end of an ACT or SCENE. (cf. D.B.O.)

Blackout sketch A short comic playlet ending with a sudden BLACKOUT to emphasise the final GAG. Popular in REVUE.

Blacks   Plain black stage drapes, usually VELOUR or SERGE.

> All black clothing worn by STAGE CREW during a performance to reduce visibility by the audience.

Black tat   Waste black fabric, useful for stapling behind LIGHT LEAKS.

Black theatre   Movement originally developed in America during the 1960's to give a voice to the Black Power Movement.

Black up   To wear black or dark MAKE-UP to perform a coloured character such as Othello. (See MINSTREL SHOW and INTEGRATED CASTING).

Blank verse   Unrhymed poetry such as is frequently found in Elizabethan drama, but also employed by some modern PLAYWRIGHTS such as T. S. Eliot (1888-1965).

Bleachers   Stepped seating units built on wheels, easily retracted to provide a clear space.

Bleed (through)   (As through a GAUZE) To gradually reduce the lighting in front of a SHARKSTOOTH GAUZE, at the same time as increasing the light behind it so that the gauze slowly becomes transparent to reveal whatever is set behind.

> Term applied to certain pigments used in scene painting which, when painted over, are difficult to cover. (Metallic silver paint may be used as a barrier to prevent this).

Blind   Used to describe a FLAT positioned where it is unseen by the audience and therefore performs only a supporting function.

Block   To plan the moves the actors will make about the stage during a performance.

> A pulley block.

Bluebell Girls   A dance troupe, dating back to the 1930's, renowned for the precision of its tall, elegant dancers. Formed and led by the indomitable "Miss Bluebell".

Board   Short for SWITCHBOARD. The central control point for stage lighting.

Boards (The)   Out of date slang for "the stage". (See TREAD THE BOARDS and GREEN.)

Boat truck   See TRUCK.

Bobbin   One of many small cylindrical carriers on a TAB TRACK for the suspension and operation of stage curtains.

Bobbinet   Lightweight netting glued onto the back of a CUT CLOTH to support heavily cut away sections.

Body stocking   Close fitting 'all-in-one' garment covering the entire body, excluding the head and hands. Usually made from cotton jersey or some other stretch fabric and frequently dyed 'flesh' colour to simulate nudity.

Bomb   (American) To FLOP.

Bomb tank   Strongly constructed metal tank or drum, open at the top and covered with strong metal mesh, used as a container for MAROONS which are electrically detonated to produce the sound of an explosion. All possible safety precautions need to be taken, and the tank should be carefully situated well away from actors or technicians.

Book (The)   The PROMPT COPY. The PROMPTER is said to be "ON THE BOOK." (cf. CARRYING THE BOOK).

The plot or dialogue sections of a musical show.

Book ceiling   A CEILING PIECE constructed as two hinged FLATS and flown by the hinged edges so that it folds face to face, thus taking up less space in the FLIES.

Book flat   (or BOOKED FLATS) Two FLATS hinged to open like a book, useful for BACKINGS.

Book wings   See WING FLATS.

Boom   Vertical scaffolding pole for mounting LANTERNS, usually set at the sides of the stage.

Border   Length of fabric or painted cloth hung horizontally above the SET as MASKING.

Boulevarde theatre   Strictly speaking, the commercial theatre of Paris, but now refers to any light, undemanding play.

Boulevardier   Actor of the type specialising in BOULEVARDE THEATRE.

Box   A small, partitioned off section of AUDITORIUM seating offering a degree of privacy and status to its occupants. Generally situated at the sides of an old style auditorium, and containing four to six movable chairs.

Short for LIGHTING BOX.

To box colours: A method used by scene painters to mix two or more buckets of paint by repeatedly pouring the paint back and forth between buckets.

Box office   The department responsible for ticket sales.

The small kiosk in the foyer of some theatres where tickets are obtained.

Good or bad box office: success or flop.

Box office returns   Statements of income received from the sale of tickets.

Box set   Stage set of a complete room with only the side nearest the audience missing. Often the SET is completed with a CEILING PIECE.

Brace   Adjustable support for FLATS. The top hooks into a screw-eye on the back of the flat, and the foot is held in place with a STAGE WEIGHT or STAGE SCREW.

A diagonal length of timber forming part of the framework of a FLAT.

Brace weight   See STAGE WEIGHT.

Braggadocio   Theatrical swagger.

Brail   To slightly divert a FLOWN piece by means of a length of rope or SASH CORD rigged to one of the FLYING LINES.

Brail line   A length of rope or SASH CORD rigged to one of the FLYING LINES to slightly divert a FLOWN piece.

Break   To stop work.

Break a leg   "Good luck". Theatre superstition dictates that the term "good luck" can in fact bring bad luck. The term originated in America but is now frequently heard all over Europe. (See TOI TOI TOI and Appendix B).

Break down   To make a PROP, costume etc. appear worn, dirty or dilapidated. (See DISTRESS).

Breast   To slightly divert a FLOWN piece by means of a separate line slung across the FLIES to deflect all the FLYING LINES supporting the piece in the desired direction.

Breast line   A length of rope or SASH CORD slung across the FLIES to deflect all the FLYING LINES supporting a FLOWN piece in the desired direction.

Breeches part   Role intended to be performed by a female artist in male costume, often found in opera. (eg. Octavian in Der Rosenkavalier).

Bridge   (LIGHTING BRIDGE) Gallery bridging the stage or auditorium to provide access to lighting equipment.

Platform installed in scenic workshops which may be raised or lowered to provide scene painters access to the top of CLOTHS etc.

Bridle   Short length of chain or cable to spread the stress on a BARREL at a suspension point.

British Council (The)   Organisation founded in 1934 to promote "British life and thought" abroad. Foreign tours of English speaking theatre are included in the Council's activities.

Broadway   The leading theatre district of America located around the Times Square section of Broadway in New York City.

Bubble   An electric light bulb.

Bubble machine   Electrically operated device to produce soap bubbles for decorative effect by passing wire loops through a soap solution.

Bums on seats   An audience.

Burlesque   Comic satire.

American VARIETY, usually including STRIPTEASE.

Burnt cork   A rough and ready means of blacking the face or suggesting facial hair.

Business   Sequences of moves or actions on stage added in rehearsal.

Business manager   See MANAGER.

Business (The)   The theatrical profession, as in "Is he in the Business?"

Busk   To improvise in emergency.

Busker   A street entertainer. From "buskin" – a type of boot often worn by tragic actors on the Elizabethan stage.

C

Cabaret   Entertainment usually presented in a restaurant, bar or night club. (See FLOOR SHOW).

Cadenza   Virtuoso passage for a solo performer in music, frequently occurring towards the end of the work and often improvised.

Cakewalk   American negro dance, so called because it was originally performed in competition for a cake.

Call   Notification of a working session. (eg. REHEARSAL CALL).

A request for an actor to come to the stage over the TANNOY system.

An acknowledgement of applause. (CURTAIN CALL).

One of four warnings that a performance is about to begin. (See HALF).

Callboard   The BACKSTAGE notice board upon which CALLS and other notices are posted.

Cans   Headphones, often with microphone attached, for communication between technicians during performances or rehearsals.

Canvas   Plain cotton fabric, usually sold already fireproofed, used to make CLOTHS and cover FLATS.

Carpet cut   Long, narrow, hinged TRAP near the front of the stage used to secure the front edge of a carpet or STAGE CLOTH.

Carrying the book   (or CARRYING THE SCRIPT) Rehearsing with the script in hand before the role had been learnt by heart.

Cast   The actors taking part in a production.

To select actors for a production.

Casting couch   Term referring to the supposed practice of some theatre directors of offering parts in return for sexual favours.

Casting directory   Publication containing lists of actors and photographs available for work, plus name of AGENT.

Cast list   List of actors and their roles in a production.

Catcall   Loud cry of disapproval or derision from the audience.

Catcher   One of a troupe of ACROBATS or AERIALISTS.

Catch phrase   Phrase associated with a particular performer or character which gains humorous effect by constant repetition. (eg. Robertson Hare's "Oh calamity!")

Cat suit   Close fitting all-in-one garment covering the body, usually excluding the hands and head. Frequently black, but may be any colour.

Catwalk   A high narrow bridge spanning the stage from one FLY FLOOR to the other.

Cavatina   Short melodious air occurring in OPERA.

Ceiling piece   Large FLAT, usually FLOWN on two or three sets of lines, covering whole or part of a BOX SET.

Ceiling plate   Metal plate with ring attached used in rigging CEILING PIECES and other items to the FLYING SYSTEM.

Centre line   Line indicated on a STAGE PLAN, and frequently marked on the stage floor, bisecting the stage from front to back.

Centre stage   The most favourable position from which a performer may dominate the stage, not necessarily the geometrical centre.

Chain   Metal chain inserted into the bottom hem of a CLOTH or GAUZE to weight it and remove wrinkles.

Chairman   COMPÈRE of Victorian and Edwardian MUSIC-HALL. Seated at a small table at the side of the stage, he introduces the ACTS using a wooden gavel to call attention.

Chalk line   See SNAP LINE

Channel   Electrical circuit used by lighting or sound systems. (See WAYS)

Charabanc trade   Organised parties of theatregoers travelling in hired motor coaches, generally considered to be unsophisticated in their responses, but welcomed by the BOX OFFICE.

Character   A role in a play or MUSICAL.

Character actor   Actor specialising in older or eccentric roles.

Character make-up   Stage MAKE-UP which alters the appearance to that of the character portrayed, usually to add age.

Character shoes   General purpose dance shoes, usually fastened with strap and button.

Charity matinee   Special afternoon performance given in aid of some deserving cause.

Charity performance   Any performance given in aid of some deserving cause.

Chaser   Device for switching a rows of light bulbs on and off consecutively in sequence for decorative effect.

Chekhovian   In the style of the Russian dramatist Anton Chekhov (1860-1904). Suggests an introspective, leisurely paced work, without a strong story-line.

Chippy   A carpenter.

Choreographer   A dance arranger.

One who makes BALLETS.

Chorus   (In Greek drama) A group of performers taking no part in the ACTION, but commenting upon it in stylised form.

Supporting singers or dancers in an OPERA or MUSICAL.

Chorus girl   A female CHORUS member, frequently chosen for looks as much as talent. Edwardian chorus girls acquired a (possibly undeserved) reputation for flirtation.

Chorus line   Row of CHORUS GIRLS performing synchronised dance routines, invariably including a sequence of HIGH KICKS.

Cinemoid   Type of GELATINE used as a colour filter for stage lighting.

Circle (The)   Upper level of AUDITORIUM seating, where the most expensive seats are usually located.

Circus   Travelling troupe of entertainers containing, among many others, ACROBATS, CLOWNS, FUNAMBULISTS and trained animals, traditionally performing in a BIG TOP.

Claque   Audience members paid to lead applause. Mainly associated with OPERA in Italy and professional rivalry between singers.

Clearing stick   Long pole with a 'T' piece at the end used for freeing FLOWN pieces when accidentally caught up. (A boat-hook is often used as a substitute).

Cleat   Single or double hook around which a rope or LINE may be temporarily tied off.

Cleat & line   Method of fastening together adjacent pieces of scenery by lashing with SASH CORD passed over a series of CLEAT HOOKS.

Cleat hook   Hook to hold a rope or LINE passed over it.

Cleat line   Length of SASH CORD fastened to the back of scenery which can be passed over a series of CLEAT HOOKS and tied off to lash pieces together.

Cloth   (or DROP) Large area of painted canvas hanging vertically.

A BACKCLOTH (or BACKDROP) completes the rear of a scene.

A CUT CLOTH has areas cut out of it to reveal scenery behind.

A FRONTCLOTH hangs DOWNSTAGE to hide a scene change taking place behind.

Clown Knock-about comic, often found in Victorian PANTOMIME and always in the CIRCUS, usually with a fantastically painted face and colourful costume. Probably the most celebrated clown was Joseph Grimaldi (1777-1837).

Coach bolts Bolt with shallow rounded head and short square section of shank immediately beneath it. It may be hammered home and the nut attached without the necessity of holding the head.

Coach screw Sturdy screw with an angular head enabling it to be used with a spanner.

Cobo Care Of Box Office.

Coconut shells Used to make the sound of horses' hooves by striking the half shells against a suitable surface.

Cold tea Traditionally substituted for whisky on stage.

Colour frame Metal frame used to hold colour filters before a LANTERN.

Colour medium Translucent material used to colour lights, now usually made from CINEMOID. (See GEL).

Colour wheel Metal disc with pieces of variously coloured GEL set into it, which, revolving before a LANTERN, changes the colour of light as the gels pass in front of the lens.

Columbine The stock maid-servant of the COMMEDIA DELL'ARTE. In the traditional English HARLEQUINADE she becomes the young girl in love with HARLEQUIN and the daughter of PANTALOON.

Comedian A comic actor. (cf. COMIC)

Comédie Française The French National Theatre, based at the Palais Royal in Paris.

Come down To end a performance – as in "what time does the show come down?"

Comedy   Play of a pleasant or humorous kind, usually with a happy ending, not necessarily intended to produce laughter.

Comedy of manners   Genre concerned mainly with satirising socially approved forms of behaviour and speech of its period. The plays of William Congreve (1670-1729) and Richard Brinsley Sheridan (1751-1816) are typical examples.

Comic   One performing, usually solo, with the main intention of producing laughter. (See STAND-UP COMIC).

Commedia dell'Arte   Form of popular theatre flourishing in Italy from the sixteenth to the eighteenth centuries. Touring troupes presented improvised COMEDY with stock characters such as Arlecchino, Pantalone, the Spanish Captain, the pedantic Doctor and many others, according to the particular talents of the company. The characters are all depicted in a notable series of etchings by the artist Jacques Callot (1592-1635). The English HARLEQUINADE and PUNCH AND JUDY shows are loosely derived from the Commedia dell'Arte.

Commercial theatre   Theatre or theatre company formed primarily for profit.

Comms   Abbr. for "communications". (See CANS).

Community theatre   Theatre group, usually amateur or a combination of amateur and professional, presenting plays based on subjects of special concern to the community in which it performs.

Company   All those involved in presenting a show or series of shows.

Company manager   See C.S.M.

Compartment batten   Trough of small, boxed FLOODLIGHTS, usually wired in three or four independent circuits and coloured with GELS, either on the stage floor, or hung above the stage for lighting a CLOTH or CYC.

Compère One who introduces the ACTS in a VARIETY show or CABARET.

Comps Complimentary seat tickets. (See PAPER).

Concert party Seaside entertainment consisting of musical and comedy items, usually on an open-air stage. (See PIERROT SHOW).

Confetti cannon Electrically detonated explosive device which fires a shower of confetti into the air.

Conjurer A stage "magician" performing solo or with an assistant; a popular entertainer from ancient times to the present day.

Conjurer's assistant An attractively dressed girl who helps the CONJURER by handing PROPS and distracting the audience's attention when required. Often "sawn in half." (cf. ILLUSIONIST).

Contact mike Small, battery operated, radio microphone which picks up sound by contact with the body.

Contract An agreement stating terms of employment. EQUITY contracts should be used whenever possible.

Copyright The right to perform a dramatic or musical work, or to use a stage design. (Note: In the U.K., no dramatic or musical work may be performed without a licence until fifty years after the death of the writer or composer, or fifty years after the first performance if this took place posthumously).

Corner (The) The PROMPT CORNER.

Corner plate Triangular piece of plywood reinforcing joints in the framework of FLATS.

Corps de ballet (French) Group of supporting dancers, in BALLET, OPERA or MUSICAL COMEDY.

Corpse To break up with laughter when acting, thereby "killing" the character portrayed.

Corsican trap   A long open TRAP running across the stage and containing a RAMP, for an actor to make an entrance from beneath the stage. First used in 1852 for the entrance of a ghost in the famous MELODRAMA *The Corsican Brothers* by Dion Boucicault (1822-90).

Coryphée   (French) Originally a male dancer, but now any dancer, who is neither a soloist nor a member of the CORPS DE BALLET.

Costume   Any clothing worn by an artist when performing. (cf. FROCKS).

Costume designer   One responsible for the visual aspects of the actors' clothing. Often the SET DESIGNER also designs costumes.

Costume drama   Play in which the actors wear period costumes.

Costume fitting   A session for individual performers to try on finished or partly finished COSTUMEs, usually attended by the COSTUME DESIGNER.

Costume parade   See DRESS PARADE.

Counterweight system   Method of flying scenery in which the flown piece is balanced by weights placed in a CRADLE running up and down in a frame at the side of the stage.

Coup de théâtre   (French) Term used to describe a sudden dramatic turn of plot, or a startling theatrical effect.

Cour   (French) Continental equivalent of STAGE LEFT. (See JARDIN).

Cover   See UNDERSTUDY.

To conceal an error, such as a memory lapse or missed entrance, by AD LIBBING.

Cradle   Suspended metal housing to carry the weights in a COUNTERWEIGHT SYSTEM.

Crash box   Container with pieces of metal and glass which, tipped into a second container, provides the sound of a crash. (See GLASS CRASH).

Creative doubling   See DOUBLING.

Crepe hair   Artificial hair supplied in the form of a tight plait to be straightened and applied with SPIRIT GUM for beards and moustaches.

Critic   One who publishes his professional view of a production in the press, on television or radio. His opinion may be influential in its success or failure.

Cross fade   To change LIGHTING STATEs by dimming the first state and increasing the new state at the same time.

Crossover   A BACKSTAGE passageway for actors and technicians to cross from one side of the stage to the other.

Crowd puller   Any production, or one aspect of a production, which attracts large audiences. This may be a popular actor, an elaborate scenic effect, or even the fact that the LEADING LADY appears naked.

Crowd scene   Scene with a large number of EXTRAS.

Crowe's Cremine   A popular theatrical MAKE-UP remover.

Crush bar   Theatre bar for the audience to gather during intervals or before a performance. (The one at the Royal Opera House in London is particularly well known).

Horizontal metal bar across an EXIT door which will unlock it when pushed. A safety precaution to avoid the public being crushed in an emergency.

C.S.M.   Company Stage Manager. One responsible for the technical administration of a theatre company. Duties include budgeting, making out schedules and arranging transport.

Cue   Any action or line of dialogue prompting a response by another actor.

Signal to initiate a change of any kind during a performance. Cues may be given through headphones, by lights or over the sound relay system. (TANNOY).

Cue lights   Small lights, usually in pairs of red and green, to give CUES to actors or technicians.

Cue to cue   Technique of cutting dialogue during a TECHNICAL REHEARSAL so that actors perform only those sections containing CUES for technical effects.

Cup and saucer school   Type of nineteenth century play performed in a realistic domestic setting. The best known is Thomas Robertson's *Caste* of 1867.

Curtain   On PLAYSCRIPTS denotes end of an act.

Curtain call   Raising of HOUSE TABS for performers to acknowledge applause. Also used in productions without HOUSE TABS, where the lighting may be faded in and out instead.

Curtain line   Line of dialogue providing the CUE for the end of a scene or Act. PANTOMIME usually ends with a RHYMING COUPLET, and there is a superstition that it is unlucky to speak it until the FIRST NIGHT. It is therefore omitted in rehearsal.

An imaginary line across the stage showing the position of the HOUSE TABS when closed. Usually marked on a STAGE PLAN.

Curtain raiser   Short play preceding the main performance, often found on 18th or 19th century PLAYBILLS.

Curtain speech   Address to the audience at the end of a performance by an actor, usually the LEADING MAN or LADY, speaking out of character.

Curtain up   The start of a performance.

Custard pie   A frequently employed missile in SLAPSTICK.

Cut   To remove lines from a script in order to shorten it.

To discard a prop, piece of scenery or effect.

Cut cloth   See CLOTH.

Cut out   Plywood FLAT or canvas DROP with areas cut away as designed.

Cutter   Member of WARDROBE staff specialising in making patterns and cutting out costumes.

Cyclorama   (Abbr. CYC.) A plain background, often curved, representing 'sky'. Sometimes built, but more frequently made of fabric hung from a BAR, extending across the full width of the stage.

D

Dais   Low ROSTRUM, to support a seat such as a throne.

Dame   A broadly comic transvestite role in PANTOMIME. Often the hero's mother, as 'Widow Twankey' in *Aladdin*. (*Cinderella* is unusual in having two Dames – the 'Ugly Sisters').

Dance belt   Crutch support worn by dancers under their costumes, usually flesh coloured.

Dancer   Exponent of any kind of dance, either male or female.

Dance routine   Sequence of dance moves of any kind, as part of a musical show or a VARIETY act.

Danseur noble   (French) Leading male dancer in classical ballet, specialising in roles such as the Prince in *Swan Lake*.

Danseuse   (French) A female dancer.

Dark   Describes a theatre during periods when there are no performances.

Darling   A term frequently used in the theatre when addressing a colleague of either sex. Not necessarily a term of endearment.

Dayman   Member of the STAGE CREW employed full time, as opposed to those working only during performances. (cf. SHOWMAN).

D.B.O.   Dead Black Out. Sudden extinguishing of all lights during a performance.

Dead   A predetermined level for a FLOWN piece. (See IN DEAD and OUT DEAD).

Scenery or PROPS no longer required in a production.

Dead line   A single LINE from the FLYING SYSTEM set at a fixed height and not required to move during the performance.

Dead spot   An ONSTAGE position where sound does not project well into the auditorium. The experienced actor will compensate for this.

Décor   Continental term for SCENERY. Sometimes pretentiously used in the U.K.

Delivery   The quality of an actor's speech.

Dénouement   Unravelling of PLOT which frequently takes place in the last scene of a play, especially a WHODUNNIT.

Designer   One responsible for visual aspects of a production, especially scenery and/or costumes.

Deus ex machina   (Latin: the god from the machine). Term deriving from ancient Greek Theatre in which mechanical devices were used to lower actors playing gods onto the stage. Now used to describe a dramatic intervention, by means of stage machinery or otherwise, often employed by the playwright to resolve a difficult situation in the PLOT.

Dexion   System of angled metal strips drilled with holes for bolting together rather like large scale 'Meccano'. Useful for constructing ROSTRA, seating units etc.

Dialect coach   One who trains actors to speak in regional or foreign dialects or accents.

Dialogue   Verbal exchanges between characters in a play.

The spoken parts of a MUSICAL or OPERETTA.

Didactic theatre   Theatrical style intended to teach a moral or political lesson.

Die   To fail. Refers either to an individual performer or an entire production.

Diffusion gel   (or FROST) Special light filter designed to spread or soften the beam of light.

Dimmer   Device to modulate the brightness of one or more LANTERNS.

Dionysos   The ancient Greek god of dramatic festivals. The Greek ORCHESTRA contained an alter to Dionysos.

Dips   Small trap doors in the stage floor providing access to electrical sockets beneath.

Director   One who conducts rehearsals and is in overall charge of the artistic interpretation of a production.

Discovered   Refers to an actor being on stage when a scene or an Act begins, giving the impression of action already in progress.

Distress   To make a PROP, costume or piece of furniture look old and worn.

Diva   A popular PRIMA DONNA.

D.L.P.   Dead Letter Perfect. Term used by actors when learning a script: Correct in every detail.

Dock   Area used for storing scenery, on or adjacent to the stage, with access to the street for moving scenery in and out of the theatre.

Dog Toby   See TOBY.

Door slam   A PRACTICAL door, equipped with locks, bolts etc., positioned out of sight of the audience to provide the sound of an OFFSTAGE door.

Double   To play two or more roles in a production. (See DOUBLING).

Double act   Any VARIETY ACT by two performers.

Double bill   Performance consisting of two short plays, operas or ballets.

Double purchase   FLYING SYSTEM in which the FLYING LINES are passed over an extra set of pulleys to provide MECHANICAL ADVANTAGE.

Double take   A comic effect indicating surprise, in which an actor throws a glance at another actor or an object, looks away, then rapidly repeats the glance, as if unable to believe his eyes. The effect is dependent on the actor's skill in TIMING.

Doubling   Two or more roles in a play performed by the same actor. This may be for reasons of economy, but may also be the result of an artistic decision. (eg. Theseus/Oberon and Hippolyta/Titania in *A Midsummer Night's Dream*). In this case it may be referred to as CREATIVE DOUBLING.

Downstage   Towards the front of the stage. (See BELOW).

Drag   Transvestite clothing. (Male or female).

Drag act   Any kind of ACT performed by one or more artists in transvestite clothing.

Drag artist   One who performs in transvestite clothing.

Drag show   A performance by transvestite artists.

Drama   Art form of ancient origins which has assumed widely varying forms throughout history. It usually implies some kind of physical embodiment of characters in a story, but its only essential ingredients are a performer and an audience, even if the audience consists of only one person.

Dramatic convention   Any unrealistic technique traditionally acceptable in a theatrical performance. (eg. SOLILOQUY and FOURTH WALL).

Dramatis personae   Latin; the persons of the drama. List of the characters in a play usually printed at the beginning of a SCRIPT.

Dramatist   One engaged in any kind of writing for the stage.

Dramaturg   One specially employed by a large theatrical company to read and advise on plays considered for production.

Drapes   Fabric hangings used as scenery, frequently VELOUR or SERGE.

Drawing room comedy   Style of COMEDY, so called because it frequently takes place in a respectable drawing room setting. Modern playwrights have rebelled against the style, but it remains popular.

Draw tabs   Stage curtains rigged on a TRACK to open and close.

Drencher   A sprinkler pipe which will spray the back of the SAFETY CURTAIN with water in the event of fire. (See SPARGE).

Dress (The)   See DRESS REHEARSAL.

Dress circle   Lowest of several upper levels of seating in an old style AUDITORIUM, so called because the audience at this level was expected to wear evening dress as in the STALLS.

Dresser   One who helps with costume care and assists with costume changes during a performance. Famous actors of the past often employed their own dressers who worked for them almost as a personal servant.

Dressing Decorative items added to a stage setting to add verisimilitude or to suggest a particular atmosphere, style or period. They may consist of anything from a vase of flowers to a cobweb.

Dressing room Room BACKSTAGE where a performer changes and otherwise prepares before going on stage.

Dress parade (or COSTUME PARADE) Time set aside for the DIRECTOR, DESIGNER and others to see finished costumes and accessories worn by actors to judge the total effect.

Dress rehearsal REHEARSAL with full scenery, lighting and costumes as at a performance, often referred to as "the dress".

Drift Distance between a FLOWN PIECE and the BAR on which it is FLOWN. A flown piece may not be attached directly to the bar, but hung from it by lengths of cable, to allow the BAR to remain out of sight when the flown piece is lowered into position.

Drift line Cable used to attach a FLOWN PIECE to the BAR on which it is FLOWN. (See DRIFT).

Drop See CLOTH.

Dry An actor forgetting his words is said to have "dried". Also referred to as "a dry".

Dry brush SCENE PAINTER'S technique using very little paint on the brush to give a textured finish.

Dry ice Frozen carbon dioxide. When dropped into a container of heated water, it will produce a thick, heavy, low-lying mist. (Dangerous to handle – gloves must be worn).

Dry ice machine Device for producing thick, heavy, low-lying clouds of mist by dropping DRY ICE into heated water.

D.S.M. Deputy Stage Manager. One in charge of rehearsals, issuing CALLS, supervising the MARK OUT, compiling the

PROMPT COPY, recording the actors' moves and notes of PROPS, also prompting if required. The D.S.M. is usually ON THE BOOK during performances.

Duet   Any musical work for two performers.

Dumb show   Mime.

Duo   Two performers of any kind regularly working together.

Dutch border   BORDER sometimes running up and down stage near the ends of the across stage borders, to complete MASKING.

Dutchman   (or DUTCHING) American equivalent of STRIPPING.

Dutch pink   Dull yellowish pigment used in scene painting.

E

Edinburgh Festival (The)   A prestigious annual Arts Festival held in Edinburgh. Many types of theatre from Britain and abroad are represented.

Edinburgh Fringe (The)   The many small unofficial events taking place around the EDINBURGH FESTIVAL. (See FRINGE).

Effects   (abbr. FX) See SPECIAL EFFECTS.

Effects wheel   Large revolving disc attached to the front of a LANTERN so that the beam passes through special holes to project the effect of clouds, rain, falling snow etc.

Electrics   (Abbr. LX). Electrical staff employed by a theatre.

Emote   To display emotion in a theatrical manner.

Encore   An extra item in a concert performed in response to audience demand.

The repetition of part of a performance in response to audience demand.

End of the pier show   Once popular sea-side entertainment consisting mainly of VARIETY ACTS, so called because it usually took place on a small stage at the far end of the pier.

End-stage   A stage positioned at one end of the AUDITORIUM with seating directly in front, but without a PROSCENIUM ARCH.

English Stage Company   See ROYAL COURT.

En pointe   (French) Balanced on the tip of the toe. A BALLET term.

ENSA   The Entertainments National Service Association. The official Forces' entertainment unit formed during World War II. Performers of all kinds visited British servicemen and performed, frequently on make-shift stages, even at the Front Line. The singer Vera Lynn was probably the most popular entertainer of this kind.

Entr'acte   A short entertainment, usually musical, taking place during the intervals between ACTS.

Entrance   To make an entrance; to enter in a theatrically effective manner.

Entrance round   A burst of applause as a performer enters.

Epic drama   Play suggesting the historical sweep of a story rather than concentrating on individual characters.

Epilogue   Speech spoken directly to the audience by an actor in character at the end of a play. (eg. Puck in *A Midsummer Night's Dream*).

Short scene at the end of a play to round off the PLOT. Bernard Shaw's Saint Joan has a well-known example.

Equity   Trade union for performers, DIRECTORS, DESIGNERS etc.

Exeunt   Latin: They go out. Used in place of EXIT when referring to more than one person.

Exit   Latin: "He (or she) goes out". Used in PLAYSCRIPTS to indicate the point where an actor leaves the stage.

A way out of the theatre. The number, size and type of exits are governed by fire regulations. They must not be obstructed and must have an illuminated sign.

Exit line   Line of dialogue spoken as, or immediately before, an actor leaves the stage.

Experimental theatre   Theatre which attempts to introduce new methods of presentation in style of acting, staging or design.

Exposition   Opening scene of a play in which the dramatist sets the PLOT in motion and indicates the situation from which it develops.

Expressionist drama   Important theatrical style of the early twentieth century which was closely allied to the Expressionist movement in art. It generally involved the use of boldly stylised gestures, scenery and costumes.

Extemporise   To perform without preparation or rehearsal, either intentionally or to cover an emergency.

Extra   Performer, having no set lines or dialogue, who appears as part of the background to the main action, as in a CROWD SCENE.

Extravaganza   A lavish entertainment of any kind.

F

Fade (in/out)   To slowly increase or decrease the level of a lighting or sound effect.

False proscenium   (Abbr. FALSE PROS) A temporary PROSCENIUM set UPSTAGE of the actual PROSCENIUM ARCH.

Fan   An enthusiast.

Fan dancer   Type of STRIPTEASE artist, who tantalisingly uses large fans to cover her (apparent) nudity.

Farce   Popular play of improbable and extravagant humour, often containing knockabout scenes. (See ALDWYCH FARCE).

Farceur   An actor specialising in playing FARCE.

Feed   (or STOOGE) Performer whose main function is to perform rehearsed dialogue with a COMEDIAN or COMIC, allowing jokes and laugh-lines to be introduced.

Female impersonator   Male artist performing in transvestite clothing, with the ability to appear convincingly feminine. (cf. DRAG ARTIST).

Feminist theatre   Movement developed in the 1960's and 70's to promote women's causes through the medium of theatre. Monstrous Regiment, a company formed in 1975, and Caryl Churchill (1938-   ) are two of the best known exponents.

Festoon   Stage curtain (TABS) with an arrangement of cords running through rings sewn to the back of the curtain to raise it in decorative swags.

Length of cable with light-bulbs attached at regular intervals, used for decorative effect.

F.E.V.   French Enamel Varnish. Strongly pigmented varnish made from aniline dyes in shellac, used for decorating PROPS, BREAKING DOWN costumes etc.

Fight arranger   One who plans the movements and rehearses the performers when any kind of fight or violent action is required in a performance.

Filled gauze   Closely woven SHARKSTOOTH GAUZE providing a good light-absorbent surface, frequently used for CYCLORAMAS.

Finale   The last scene in a VARIETY show or MUSICAL, usually of a spectacular nature, offering an opportunity for the performers to acknowledge applause.

Fire   A word which, to avoid panic, should never be used in an emergency. Most theatres have a special code word to be used instead.

Fire exit   Any exit may be designated a FIRE EXIT by the local Fire Officer. It must not be locked or obstructed during a performance, and must be clearly indicated by an illuminated sign.

Fireproofing   All scenery, PROPS and DRAPES must be adequately fireproofed. The local Fire Officer may check before a performance, and he has the power to cancel the show if he is not satisfied. (See FLAMEBAR).

First night nerves/jitters   Natural nervous tension felt at the first performance. It can be responsible for generating a special excitement which is often difficult to recapture subsequently.

Fishnets   TIGHTS made from an open mesh, usually black or flesh colour. Very flattering to the legs and consequently frequently worn by female dancers, SHOWGIRLS and PRINCIPAL BOYS in PANTOMIME.

Fit up   (or SET UP) To install, or the physical embodiment of, a production's scenery and lighting on the stage.

Fit up company   Travelling company, common in the nineteenth century, erecting its own dismantlable stage and scenery to provide cheap, popular plays.

Five & nine   Reference numbers of light (5) and dark (9) flesh coloured GREASEPAINT sticks, used in combination to provide a tinted base for stage MAKE-UP, now generally replaced by PANCAKE make-up.

Flamebar   A commonly used FIREPROOFING medium.

Flash box   Small metal box containing specially prepared combustible material to be electrically detonated to produce an explosive flash, and usually, a cloud of smoke.

Flat   Rectangular timber frame, covered with canvas or plywood, generally used to form the walls of a BOX SET.

Flicker wheel   Metal wheel, containing open slots, revolved in front of a LANTERN to create a flickering effect.

Flies   Area above the stage into which scenery can be hoisted out of view of the audience.

Flipper   Small, flat piece of scenery hinged to a larger one.

Float   (As in "to float a flat") To drop a FLAT to the floor in such a way that it lands gently, cushioned by the air.

Floats   See FOOTLIGHTS.

Flood   Large, non-focusing LANTERN providing a wash of light.

Floor cloth   See STAGE CLOTH.

Floor show   Caberet type entertainment, usually on a dance floor.

Flop   A production which is disastrously unsuccessful.

Flown   Suspended on LINES from the GRID.

Fluff   A verbal slip: hence "To fluff a LINE."

Flyer   (or FLIER) Advertising leaflet for general distribution.

Fly floor   (or FLY GALLERY) High working platform at the side of the stage from which FLY LINES are operated.

Fly in   To lower scenery into view of the audience.

Flying harness   Strongly made structure of leather straps with a device for attaching special FLYING LINES at the back or sides. Worn by an actor beneath his costume when he is required to be FLOWN, as in J. M. Barrie's play *Peter Pan.*

Flying iron   Flat metal strip with a hinged ring screwed to the back of a FLOWN piece to attach FLY LINES.

Flying space   The amount of space available in the FLY TOWER above the stage for use by the FLYING SYSTEM.

Flying system   Method of suspending scenery or lighting equipment above the stage, now frequently COUNTERWEIGHTED.

Fly line   (or FLYING LINE) A rope or cable used to suspend scenery from the GRID.

Flyman   Technician who operates the scenery suspension system.

Fly out   To raise scenery out of view of the audience.

Fly rail   Rail on the side of the FLY FLOOR with CLEATS for securing hemp FLY LINES.

Fly tower   High architectural structure built above the stage to contain the FLIES.

Focus   To adjust beams of SPOTLIGHTS and the directions in which they point.

F.O.H.   See FRONT OF HOUSE.

Fold back   Sound system including speakers placed specially for the benefit of the performers, so that they can hear the accompanying instruments above the sound of their own voice or instrument.

Follies   Lavish type of VARIETY show named after the Ziegfeld Follies staged yearly in New York by Florenz Ziegfeld (1876-1932).

Follow spot   SPOTLIGHT moved by an operator to light a performer as he moves about the stage.

Foot   (As in "to foot a flat") To place the foot at the base of a FLAT to prevent it slipping when being raised or lowered.

Footlights   Series of LANTERNS set in a row along the front edge of the stage floor.

Forestage   See APRON.

Fourth wall   The imaginary wall of a BOX SET, assumed to be between the actors and the audience.

Foyer Area used by the public inside a theatre's main entrance, usually containing the BOX OFFICE.

Freak show A fairground sideshow, now obsolete, in which people and animals with spectacular deformities were exhibited. These included bearded ladies, Siamese twins, midgets, two-headed sheep and many others, often fake.

French brace Fixed wooden support hinged to a FLAT.

French farce (See FARCE) The French version of the genre is rather more exaggerated than the English, and usually more risqué.

French flat (or FRENCHMAN) A large FLAT or RUN of flats battened together and FLOWN, typically forming the rear wall of a SET.

Frenchman See FRENCH FLAT.

French's Acting Edition PLAYSCRIPT published by Samuel French Ltd., usually containing STAGE DIRECTIONS and notes of PROPS and effects.

Fresnel lens Lens with a stepped moulding to soften the edges of the light beam.

Fresnel (spot) LANTERN giving a soft edged pool of light.

Fringe (The) (or FRINGE THEATRE) Performances taking place away from the main centres of theatrical activity. The term was first used to describe the many small unofficial theatrical events taking place around the EDINBURGH FESTIVAL. The EDINBURGH FRINGE has now expanded so much that terms "Fringe of the Fringe" or "Fringe Fringe" are used. Certain PUB THEATRES in London, such as The Bush, The King's Head, and The Old Red Lion have established reputations for high standards of new writing and production. (cf. OFF BROADWAY).

Frocks COSTUMES – male or female.

Frontcloth See CLOTH.

Front of House   (Abbr. F.O.H.) Parts of the theatre open to the public.

Front of house manager   See HOUSE MANAGER.

Front of house staff   Programme sellers, usherettes, BOX OFFICE staff, bar staff, cleaners and lavatory attendants.

Frost   See DIFFUSION GEL.

F.U.F.   Full Up to Finish. Increasing the intensity of light during the last few bars of a musical number to attract greater applause.

Fullers' earth   Aluminium silicate. A greyish powder used to BREAK DOWN costumes and simulate loose dust on books, furniture etc.

Funambulist   A tightrope walker.

F.X.   See SPECIAL EFFECTS.

G

Gaiety Girl   A singer and/or dancer performing at the Gaiety Theatre in the Strand, London, at the end of the nineteenth century. A popular series of REVUES were presented, each with the word "girl" in the title. The "girls" were noted for their liveliness and good looks.

Gaffer tape   Wide, heavy duty, canvas backed adhesive tape with a great variety of general uses.

Gag   A joke, either verbal or visual.

To insert humorous AD-LIBS to raise laughs.

Gala performance   A Special celebratory performance to commemorate some special event or in honour of a notable person.

Gallery   Highest and cheapest level of AUDITORIUM seating.

Gang show   Show presented and performed by Boy Scouts.

Gate leg (rostrum)   Collapsible ROSTRUM with removable top and folding 'gate'-like supports.

Gauze   Suspended CLOTH made of fine mesh, which, when lit from the front appears to be opaque, but which becomes transparent when scenery or actors behind the gauze are lit, and light is removed from the front. (See SHARKSTOOTH.)

Gay Sweatshop   Company of homosexual actors presenting plays on homosexual themes.

Gel   (JELLY) Abbr. for GELATINE. Transparent colour medium set in front of a LANTERN to colour the light. (No longer actually made from gelatine).

Gelatine   See GEL.

Gel frame   See COLOUR FRAME.

Genesius (Saint)   Patron Saint of actors. His Feast Day falls on 25th August. According to tradition, after playing before the Roman emperor Diocletian, Genesius declared that during the performance he had been converted to Christianity. He was tortured and eventually decapitated. The story is probably fictitious.

Gerb   PYROTECHNIC device, electrically detonated, to produce a large flash and explosion.

Get in   The taking of scenery, PROPS, costumes etc. into the theatre.

Get off   OFFSTAGE steps providing access to a ROSTRUM or upper level of a SET.

Get out   Removal from the theatre of all scenery, PROPS, costumes etc. associated with a production.

Ghost   An unwanted beam of light leaking from a LANTERN.

As in "Has the ghost walked?" – meaning "Has the manager been round with the pay?" There is a tradition that Shakespeare himself played the role of the ghost in

Hamlet. The ghost has a long wait between entrances during which he may have collected the takings and paid the actors.

Gig A single performance by a band or pop group.

Gimmick Any kind of attention catching device adopted by a performer, such as the shabby suit worn by Charlie Chaplin.

Any secret gadget used by a CONJURER to perform a trick.

Glass crash Bucket containing pieces of metal and broken glass which, when tipped into a second container, provides the sound of breaking glass. (cf. CRASH BOX).

Glitter Very small pieces of reflective material glued to scenery or PROPS for a sparkling effect. Available in silver, gold and various colours.

Globe (The) The Elizabethan theatre on the south bank of the Thames in London where Shakespeare worked. A few remains have recently been discovered, but little is known for certain about its structure.

Glove puppet (or HAND PUPPET) PUPPET worn on the hand, the arms and head being operated by the fingers and thumb. PUNCH AND JUDY are glove puppets.

Glue size See SIZE.

Gobo Thin metal plate with a design cut into it, which, when placed in front of a LANTERN, projects the design onto the stage. Typically used for the effect of light striking through a window or foliage.

Gods (The) Seats in the highest part of the AUDITORIUM in an old fashioned theatre. Also refers to those members of the audience occupying them, as in "playing to the gods".

Go up Start the show, as in "what time do we go up?", referring to the raising of HOUSE TABS.

Graining Scene painting technique in which pigment is dragged streakily over a surface in imitation of wood grain.

Grand drape (American) The HOUSE TABS.

Grand guignol Dramatic genre originating in nineteenth century Paris (Théâtre du Grand Guignol), consisting of short plays containing murder, mutilation, rape and various other horrors calculated to thrill the audience.

Grand Master A switch or DIMMER controlling all circuits in use.

Grand opera Large scale OPERA containing no spoken dialogue, such as the operas of Richard Wagner (1813-1883) and Giuseppe Verdi (1813-1901).

Grand pas de deux A virtuoso dance sequence for two leading dancers (male and female) occuring in most classical ballets.

Gravel tray Tray of gravel placed on the stage floor out of sight of the audience, used by actors to give the sound of approaching footsteps.

Grave trap TRAP near centre stage, usually about 1m x 2m, often used as a grave, as in *Hamlet*, Act 5, sc.1.

Greasepaint Theatrical MAKE-UP in the form of sticks of pigment bound with grease.

Greek theatre Usually refers to the theatre of ancient Greece from the sixth century B.C. The theatres were large AMPITHEATRES and plays were associated with religious festivals. COMEDY and TRAGEDY were both performed, and the plays conformed to strict theatrical conventions. (See UNITIES).

Green Stage. (Cockney rhyming slang – 'Greengage').

The colour green is traditionally unlucky when used on stage, either for SETS or COSTUMES.

Green room The actors' relaxation room BACKSTAGE. The reason for the name is obscure, but may be simply that the original Green Room at the Theatre Royal, Drury Lane, London, was painted green.

Grelco A two-way 15 amp electrical adapter.

Grid Strong timber or metal framework just below the stage roof, supporting the FLYING SYSTEM.

Groove system A mechanical method of changing scenery in view of the audience, in use from the 17th to late 19th centuries, in which FLATS slid along special slots cut into the stage floor. Some very old theatres still retain traces of the system.

Ground plan See STAGE PLAN.

Groundrow Long, low piece of scenery, typically profiled and painted as hills, roof-tops etc.

Series of LANTERNS set in a row on the stage floor for lighting the bottom of CLOTHS, and scenic groundrows.

Grouping Placing performers about the stage to present an attractive stage picture – especially important in scenes containing a number of EXTRAS.

Grummet Metal plate with a loop, screwed to the back of a FLOWN piece to act as a guide for a FLYING LINE threaded through it.

Guest artist Performer appearing, usually in a leading role, with a company of which he is not a regular member.

Guignol Traditional French GLOVE PUPPET figure, enjoying much the same popularity as PUNCH in Britain.

H

Hair lace Fine, flesh coloured gauze at the front edge of a wig, used to make the hair of the wig appear to grow naturally from the skin. Also used as a base for false moustaches and beards.

Half (The) CALL given to actors half an hour before they will be called to the stage to begin a performance, ie. at 35 minutes before the advertised starting time. Subsequent calls are the 'quarter' (at 20 minutes), 'five minutes' (at 10 minutes) and 'beginners' (at 5 minutes).

Ham Derogatory term referring to a heavily exaggerated style of acting or its exponent. There is a tradition that the term derives from Ham House near Richmond, which was thought to be greatly over-decorated. Alternatively, it is suggested that it may be an abbreviation for 'hamfatter', from an old Negro minstrel song, *The Hamfat Man*.

Ham it up To act in a deliberately exaggerated way.

Hamlet wait A prolonged period spent OFFSTAGE by an actor during a play, such as that which occurs for the actor playing Hamlet between Act 4, sc.3 and Act 5, sc.1.

Hand prop See PERSONAL PROP.

Hand puppet See GLOVE PUPPET.

Hanging iron Flat metal strip formed into a hook at one end, screwed to the back of a FLAT to attach FLYING LINES.

Rectangular metal plate with a fixed ring, screwed to the back of a FLOWN piece to attach FLYING LINES.

Hard masking MASKING consisting of FLATS, as opposed to DRAPES.

Harlequin Hero of the traditional HARLEQUINADE, in love with COLUMBINE. He traditionally wears a costume patterned in multicoloured diamond shapes.

Harlequinade An important element in Victorian PANTOMIME, in which the story was temporarily suspended for the introduction of a sequence involving characters such as HARLEQUIN, COLUMBINE, PANTALOON and CLOWN, with dances, SLAPSTICK and special scenic tricks. Extremely popular in its day, it is hardly ever seen nowadays.

Haystack lantern   See LANTERN.

Head block   Device containing three or more pulleys on a common shaft which, set onto the GRID, brings together all the FLYING LINES in one set and diverts them to the FLY GALLERY.

Heads!   Frequently heard cry of warning. Theatre technicians are often required to work above the heads of others, either in the FLYS or on ladders. "Heads!" should be called out automatically whenever anything is being lowered to the stage or when an object is accidentally dropped.

Hemp house   Theatre with a rope and pulley FLYING SYSTEM (cf. COUNTERWEIGHTED FLYING SYSTEM).

Hemps   Uncounterweighted, rope FLYING LINES, referring to the hemp ropes used before manila ropes became available.

High comedy   Sophisticated comedy (cf. LOW COMEDY).

High kick   Spectacular self-descriptive dance step traditionally performed by a CHORUS LINE.

Histrionics   Play acting.

Hit   A very successful production.

Hoofer   (American) Dancer of either sex, especially a CHORUS dancer.

Hook clamp   Metal device for fixing a LANTERN to a BAR.

Hoop   Large semi-rigid loop of wire, cane or corset-boning worn beneath a costume to hold out the skirt, especially with period dresses such as the crinoline.

Hooped stockings   (or TIGHTS) Tights or stockings with bold horizontal stripes running around the leg such as those traditionally worn by a PANTOMIME DAME.

House   The audience, as in "a good House."

House curtain/tabs   The permanent curtain set just behind the PROSCENIUM ARCH, also known as the RAG.

House lights   AUDITORIUM lighting.

House manager   (or FRONT OF HOUSE MANAGER) One responsible for running all parts of the theatre to which the audience is admitted, including the BOX OFFICE, bars and toilets as well as the AUDITORIUM.

House seats   Small number of seats set aside at each performance for use by members of the theatre's management or special guests.

House tabs   See HOUSE CURTAIN.

Hurry music   Rapid musical accompaniment suggesting speed or haste, traditionally associated with Victorian MELODRAMA.

I

Ice show   Show taking place on an ice covered ARENA, with performers carrying out graceful and spectacular musical routines on ice skates.

Illusionist   CONJURER specialising in large scale effects, such as sawing a lady in half.

Impresario   A PRODUCER.
   Manager of an OPERA or BALLET company.

Impressionist   One who imitates the voice and/or mannerisms of famous people.

Improvisation   Spontaneous and unrehearsed reaction to a situation. A technique often used by actors when developing a role, but also used by PLAYWRIGHTS as a basis for constructing a scene or an entire play.

In dead   A predetermined level for a FLOWN piece when lowered into position on stage.

Ingénue   Young female role, usually an artless or innocent type.

Inset Small scene set within a larger one.

Interlude Short piece of music or light drama performed between the ACTS of a longer work.

Intermission See INTERVAL.

Interpretation The particular manner in which an actor, singer or dancer chooses to perform his role.

Interval (or INTERMISSION) A break between ACTS, usually of about fifteen or twenty minutes. Unusually lengthy works, such as the operas of Richard Wagner (1813-1883), may have an interval as long as an hour or eighty minutes, to give the audience time for a meal.

Iris Circular shutter which may be adjusted to vary the width of the beam given by a PROFILE SPOT.

Iron The fireproof SAFETY CURTAIN immediately behind the PROSCENIUM ARCH.

Isora SKY CLOTH or CYCLORAMA made from a translucent plastic to be lit from behind.

I.W.B. Internally Wired BARREL.

J

Jacobean drama Plays written during the reign of James I (1603-25), a fertile period in British drama. The term usually implies a TRAGEDY of a dark or melodramatic nature. Playwrights of the period include John Webster (? -1634), Ben Jonson (1572-1637), Thomas Middleton (1570-1627) and Thomas Dekker (c.1572-c.1632).

Jardin (French) Continental equivalent of STAGE RIGHT. (See COUR).

Jelly See GEL.

Jingle heels TAP SHOES with loosely fitted, double metal plates at the heel, providing a double tap each time the heel hits the floor.

Juggler   Popular VARIETY or CIRCUS performer who demonstrates skill in throwing and catching various objects such as balls, clubs, batons or plates, keeping several in the air at once.

Juliet balcony   A small opening or balcony at an upper level DOWNSTAGE of the PROSCENIUM ARCH, such as may be used for the balcony scene in *Romeo and Juliet.*

Juvenile   (Abbr. JUV or JUVE) A young actor of either sex.

Juvenile drama   TOY THEATRE performances. (See POLLOCK'S).

Juvenile lead   Actor (or actress) specialising in playing young leading role(s), frequently a lover or hero.

K

Kabuki   Popular traditional form of Japanese theatre, employing elaborate styles of acting and staging. (cf. NO DRAMA).

Kensington Gore   Type of artificial blood. (After the London thoroughfare of the same name).

Kill   To switch off a LANTERN or effect.

Kitchen sink   A term coined in the late 1950's to describe a realistic dramatic style reacting against the popular DRAWING-ROOM COMEDY of the period. The trend began with *Look Back In Anger* by John Osborne, produced at the ROYAL COURT in 1956.

Knockabout farce   Type of FARCE mainly based upon physical misfortune, eg. falling over or being hit by missiles such as CUSTARD PIES.

L

Ladder   Ladder-shaped metal framework hanging at the sides of the stage to support LANTERNS for side lighting. Not intended to be used for climbing.

Lamp   See LANTERN.

Lantern   (or LUMINAIRE or LAMP) An individual item of stage lighting equipment.

Air-vent or skylight in the roof of the theatre above the GRID. (HAYSTACK LANTERN).

Last night   The final performance.

Leading man/lady   (Abbr. MALE or FEMALE LEAD) Actor or actress performing the main male or female role in a play, usually implying an experienced actor, older than a JUVENILE.

Leaf border   See TREE BORDER.

Légerdemain   Sleight-of-hand. Conjuring, especially that depending upon digital dexterity.

Legitimate   (Abbr. LEGIT) Term used to refer to the dramatic stage, as opposed to MUSIC HALL, VARIETY etc.

Legs   Lengths of fabric hanging vertically to MASK the sides of the stage.

Leg show   Any musical show containing attractive girls wearing costumes designed to show off the legs.

Leko   (American) General term for a PROFILE SPOT.

Leotard   Close fitting garment often worn with TIGHTS, made from cotton jersey or other stretch fabric, and covering the body apart from the legs, head and hands.

Level   Degree of intensity of a LANTERN or volume of a sound effect.

ROSTRUM or raised area of the stage.

Librettist   One who writes the words of an OPERA or other musical show, usually working in close co-operation with the composer.

Libretto   The words of an OPERA or other musical show. (cf. SCORE).

Life mask   Cast taken from a performer's face used as a base upon which to model a MASK or PROSTHESIS.

Lift   Stage floor section which may be raised or lowered.

In dance, a movement involving lifting a partner.

Lifts   Wedge shaped pieces of cork sometimes worn by a performer inside the heels of his shoes to add height.

Light curtain   Low voltage, downward-pointing lighting units hung in a row above the stage to create a 'curtain' of visible light beams.

Lighting   Arrangement and modulation of LANTERNS. An important aspect of any production, not only allowing performers to be seen by the audience, but also adding mood and atmosphere to a scene.

Lighting batten   See BATTEN.

Lighting box   See BOX.

Lighting bridge   See BRIDGE.

Lighting designer   One responsible for the overall lighting effects and the arrangement and modulation of LANTERNS for a production. (See LIGHTING).

Lighting plot   List of lighting changes in a performance with notes of CUES.

Lighting rig   See RIG.

Lighting state   Predetermined set of light levels.

Light leak   Light seeping through a join between two FLATS or through thin canvas. Rectified by stapling BLACK TAT to the back, or painting the back of the canvas black.

Light tower   Tall metal framed structure to support LANTERNS.

Limes   FOLLOW SPOTS — From 'limelight', an intense white light used for special effects during the nineteenth century.

Line   A single piece of spoken dialogue.

A rope or cable from the GRID.

Length of SASH CORD used to CLEAT a FLAT.

Line rehearsal   Rehearsal called solely for actors to practise speaking the text from memory.

Lining stick   Wooden lath with a bevelled edge and a handle used by scene painters for ruling straight lines.

Linnebach cyc.   Type of CYCLORAMA, named after its inventor Adolf Linnebach, suspended from a curved TRACK so that it can be drawn across the stage to be stored in a vertical roll at the side.

Linnebach projector   Device used to project an image from a slide onto scenery, developed by Adolf Linnebach.

Literary agent   One who helps a writer to find a publisher or a PRODUCER for his work, negotiates contracts, and gives advice in return for a percentage of the profits.

Loading floor   See LOADING GALLERY.

Loading gallery   High platform at the side of the stage, above the FLY FLOOR, for loading COUNTERWEIGHTS into the CRADLE.

Lock off   To tighten the screws used to adust the angle and focus of a LANTERN to avoid accidental slippage.

Lord Chamberlain   The government official authorised to censor all theatrical productions from 1737 until the Theatre Act of 1968.

Louvred ceiling   A scenic CEILING made in long sections running across stage and hung so that the DOWNSTAGE edge of each section is higher than the UPSTAGE edge to permit lighting through the gaps.

Low comedy   Type of coarse FARCE employing SLAPSTICK and bawdy humour.

Luminaire   Internationally used term for any kind of lighting instrument.

L.X.   See ELECTRICS.

Lyrics   The words of a song or the sung parts of a MUSICAL.

M

Magician   CONJURER or ILLUSIONIST.

Make-up   Most performers of either sex wear make-up of some kind when on stage, as the multiple sources of light tend to wipe out natural shadows. However its use has steadily declined in recent years due to improvements in stage lighting and a more realistic form of drama. (See CHARACTER MAKE-UP, PANCAKE and FIVE AND NINE).

Manager   Administrator who runs the business or commercial side of a theatre.

Marie Tempest   Improvised device made from a cord and a weight to ensure that a stage door will remain either open or closed as desired.

Marionette   Puppet operated by strings from above.

Mark   Small piece of coloured adhesive tape or paint on the stage floor to indicate the correct position of a piece of scenery, furniture etc.

To rehearse using restricted voice or movements to conserve energy.

Mark out   (or MARK UP) A full-sized plan of the SET drawn on the floor with adhesive tape or paint for rehearsals.

To outline a design on scenery prior to painting.

Maroon   Electrically detonated explosive device to produce an OFFSTAGE explosion. It must always be used in a BOMB TANK with appropriate safety precautions.

Mask   To hide OFFSTAGE areas, LANTERNS etc. from view.

Moulded covering worn to disguise the face or to suggest change of identity.

Masking   Scenic elements which primarily perform the function of hiding OFFSTAGE areas, LANTERNS etc. from view of the audience.

An actor blocking the audience's view of another actor.

Masque   Formal dramatic entertainment popular at Renaissance courts presented by masked performers, usually containing songs and dance.

Master   Electrical switch which will override all other switches.

Master of Ceremonies   (Abbr. M.C.) Originally a court official responsible for entertainments, now generally refers to a MUSIC HALL COMPÈRE or CHAIRMAN.

Matinée   A daytime performance.

Matinée idol   A popular good looking actor, especially attractive to MATINÉE audiences.

M.D.   Musical Director.

Mechanical advantage   Method of reducing the weight of FLOWN pieces by including an extra set of pulleys in the FLYING SYSTEM.

Melodrama   Originally a play with musical accompaniment, but now referring to a type of sensational drama of generally crude sentimentality especially popular in Victorian times. (e.g. *The Bells* first presented by Sir Henry Irving (1838-1905) at the Lyceum Theatre in 1871).

Memory board   Computerised lighting control system which "remembers" the required LEVEL of each LANTERN at every change and recalls them electronically at the touch of a button.

Method (The)   (or METHOD ACTING) See ACTORS' STUDIO.

Metteur en scène   (French) Theatrical DIRECTOR.

Mike   (or MIC) Abbr. microphone.

Mime To act without spoken words, or a performer who uses this technique, eg. Marcel Marceau (1923-).

Minstrel The professional entertainer of the Middle Ages, usually itinerant, but sometimes permanently attached to some noble household.

Minstrel show Musical entertainment which became popular in the mid-1800's. The (invariably white) performers blackened their faces in a stylised Negro impersonation. The black and white minstrels were popular in 1950's and 1960's on stage and television.

Mirror ball Electrically revolving sphere covered in pieces of mirror. When SPOTLIGHTS are directed onto it, small, swiftly moving spots of light are reflected to decorative effect.

Mirror scrim Flexible plastic mirror used in the same manner as SHARKSTOOTH GAUZE, i.e. it may be rendered transparent by a change in lighting.

Mis en scène (Continental) The staging of a production.

Mixer Device for adding together sound from two or more sources and routing it to one or more outputs, also for 'processing' sound in volume or tonal quality.

Model See SET MODEL.

Monkey stick Rod attached to a CLEAT LINE so that the line may be easily and noiselessly slipped over the top CLEAT, without 'throwing'. (cf. THROW A LINE).

Monologue A long speech for a solo performer, designed to entertain and display the performer's skill; in a play, an extended solo passage, sometimes the entire play (monodrama), i.e. *Krapp's Last Tape* by Samuel Beckett (1906-89).

Motley Coarse cloth in various colours, used for the traditional dress of Elizabethan fools or jesters, now a general term for stage wear.

Move   Any planned and rehearsed action made by an actor during a performance.

Mugging   To pull faces in an effort to raise laughs, possibly deriving from the grotesque face on a Toby jug.

Multiple set   Stage SETTING which contains several locations all visible at the same time as in Tennessee William's *A Streetcar Named Desire*. The Medieval MYSTERY PLAY used an early form of multiple set.

Mummers   Originally, amateur performers of traditional folk plays, especially at Christmas. Nowadays, often used as a derogatory term for, and by, actors.

Musical comedy   (or MUSICAL) Popular form of entertainment in which singing and dancing are combined with a dramatic plot. Rodgers and Hammerstein in America, and Ivor Novello and Andrew Lloyd Webber in the U.K., are well known as writers and composers of the genre.

Music-hall   Popular working-class VARIETY entertainment of the nineteenth century.

A theatre building specially dedicated to such entertainment.

Mystery play   Medieval religious drama traditionally performed by amateur players at the Feast of Corpus Christi on a procession of decorated wagons travelling from place to place. The plays usually depicted the fall and redemption of man, finishing with the last judgment, and "dammed souls" being cast into Hell.

N

National Theatre (The)   Now The Royal National Theatre. Theatre company founded by Sir Laurence Olivier in 1963, based, since 1976, in its own building in London's South Bank arts complex.

Nativity play   Religious play depicting the story of the birth of Christ, usually performed at Christmas.

NATTKE   National Association of Theatrical, Television and Kine Employees. Trade union for all theatre technicians.

Naturalism   Performance presented as realistically as possible by careful attention to detail. (cf. REALISM.)

Net   See BOBBINET.

No drama   (or NOH) Classical form of Japanese theatre, with heavily stylised acting and staging.

Noises off   OFFSTAGE SOUND EFFECTS.

Nose putty   Malleable plastic material for building false noses, warts, scars etc. directly onto the face.

Notes   Constructive comments made by the DIRECTOR to actors and technicians after a rehearsal or performance.

A session at which such comments are made.

Notices   Press REVIEWS of a production.

Number   Song or dance routine in a MUSICAL or VARIETY show.

O

Oberammergau   Village in Bavaria where a play depicting the life of Christ is performed by the local population every ten years. The play was first performed during an outbreak of plague in 1633.

Off   Refers to an actor failing to enter at the correct time, forcing actors ONSTAGE to COVER.

Off Broadway   The small AVANT-GARDE theatres set up as an alternative to the major commercial theatres of BROADWAY.   The terms "off-off Broadway" and even "off-off-off Broadway" are sometimes used. (cf FRINGE).

Offstage   Any position out of view of the audience.

Old Stagers (The)   The oldest amateur dramatic society in the U.K. Based in Canterbury, it was founded in 1842.

Old time music-hall   Type of musical entertainment in which the audience, often dressed in period costume, is encouraged to join in the choruses of popular songs. Items are traditionally introduced by a CHAIRMAN in imitation of Victorian or Edwardian MUSIC-HALL.

One-acter   Short play consisting of one ACT only. Two or three one-acters will often be performed in one evening.

One-liner   Humorous remark neatly expressed in one short line of dialogue.

Onstage   Any position within the ACTING AREA.

On the book   See BOOK.

On the road   Touring.

O.P.   Opposite Prompt. Stage right – from an actor's viewpoint when facing the audience (cf. P.S.).

Open air theatre   Any performance taking place in the open air, often in a specially constructed enclosure, such as the Open Air Theatre in Regent's Park, London, founded by Sydney Carroll in 1933.

Open dress (rehearsal)   A DRESS REHEARSAL usually taking place before an invited audience.

Opening night   The first performance.

Opera   Music drama. (see GRAND OPERA).

Opera bouffe   (French) OPERETTA.

Operetta   Type of light OPERA usually based on a romantic plot in a glamorous setting. Franz Lehar's *The Merry Widow*, first performed in 1906, is typical of the genre.

Orchestra　Musicians accompanying a performance.

Large circular area in the theatres of ancient Greece occupied by a CHORUS of dancers. (See DIONYSOS).

Orchestra pit　Sunken area immediately in front of the stage occupied by musicians accompanying a musical show, often partly recessed beneath the stage.

Orchestra stalls　Auditorium seating at the front of the STALLS, nearest to the ORCHESTRA.

O.T.T.　Over The Top. Greatly exaggerated or overdone.

Out dead　Predetermined level for a flown piece when raised to its 'rest' position above the stage.

Overact　To perform in an inappropriately exaggerated manner.

Overture　Orchestral introduction to a musical performance.

Overture and beginners please!　CALL given five minutes before the start of a musical show to request opening performers to take their places ONSTAGE.

P

P.A.　The Public Address sound system.

Pace　Speed at which a scene or a play is performed – of crucial importance to a successful production. The term does not imply a constant speed, but one which varies considerably from scene to scene.

Pack　Pile of FLATS stacked in the WINGS or SCENE DOCK ready for use.

Pageant　Strong, slightly diffused, directional LANTERN, nowadays generally replaced by a soft-edge SPOT.

Open air festival performance, usually based upon a historical subject.

Wagon upon which MYSTERY PLAYS were performed.

Paint bridge Platform running the width of the PAINT FRAME, often built to be easily raised and lowered, so that painters may reach all parts of the scenery on the frame.

Paint frame Large vertical frame to which scenery is nailed for painting. Sometimes the frame may be raised and lowered so that painters may reach all parts of the scenery on the frame. (See PAINT BRIDGE).

Pan To operate a piece of lighting equipment so that the beam moves from side to side.

(Abbr. panatrope). A record turntable, now obsolete.

Pancake Non-greasy, water soluble MAKE-UP base.

Pantaloon A comic old man, often COLUMBINE'S father or husband in the traditional HARLEQUINADE.

Paper To provide free seats to increase the size of the audience, as in "to paper the house".

PAR Planed All Round, or finished on all sides. Term used when buying timber.

Parcan LANTERN to hold a PAR LAMP.

Par lamp Lamp containing its own optical system, producing a nearly parallel beam.

Pas de deux (French) Dance for two performers, especially in BALLET. (Also pas de trois, pas de quatre etc.)

Pass door Door providing access between the auditorium and the stage.

Passerelle Catwalk used by SHOWGIRLS, passing from one side of the stage to the other around the front of the ORCHESTRA PIT, often specially lit from beneath.

Passion play Religious play depicting the events surrounding the Crucifixion of Christ, popular in Medieval times, and still occasionally performed. (See MYSTERY PLAY and OBERAMMERGAU.)

Patch   To link DIMMERS to appropriate circuits.

Patch board   (or PATCH PANEL) Device to change the circuits affected by individual DIMMERS, thus greatly increasing the flexibility of the lighting system.

Patron saint of actors   See GENESIUS.

Patter   Words spoken, to accompany the action of a VARIETY ACT, especially a CONJURER, often comic.

Patter-song   Comic song in which many words are spoken or sung as quickly as possible.

Pebble convex spot   (or P.C. SPOT) Similar to a FRESNEL SPOT, but producing a beam with a harder edge and, therefore, less SCATTER.

Pelmet clip   Gadget used for temporarily attaching a small built object, such as a pelmet or shelf, to the face of a piece of scenery. It consists of two metal plates, one with a slot, screwed to the larger piece, and the other with a metal 'button' screwed to the smaller piece so that the 'button' may be engaged in the slot.

Penny gaff   Cheap nineteenth century theatre catering for the poorer classes.

Penny plain, twopence coloured   Small printed sheets of scenery and characters for use inTOY THEATRES popular in the nineteenth century. They were usually sold for one penny each uncoloured and twopence each already coloured by hand. (See POLLOCK'S).

Peoria (it won't play in)   (American) Too sophisticated.

Pepper's ghost   Stage trick popular in the nineteenth century whereby a hidden actor playing a ghost is reflected by a large sheet of glass positioned at an angle upon the stage, and so appears to be transparent.

Perch   Position for hanging LANTERNS, situated above head height, behind the side of the PROSCENIUM.

Vertical opening in a side wall of the AUDITORIUM in which LANTERNS are hung.

Plate   71

Periaktoi   Three FLATS set in the form of a prism on a revolving base, often used to change WING FLATS quickly and smoothly, thought to originate from the classical Greek theatre.

Personal prop   (See HAND PROP).

Photo call   Session arranged to take publicity photographs of performers appearing in a production, usually in full COSTUME and MAKE-UP.

Piano wire   Very strong wire, almost invisible from the audience, used to FLY scenery where FLYING LINES will be in view.

Pierrette   A female PIERROT.

Pierrot   A simple-minded character deriving from the COMMEDIA DELL'ARTE, traditionally wearing a loose white costume with long sleeves and a frill at the neck.

A performer in a PIERROT SHOW.

Pierrot show   Seaside entertainment, consisting of musical and comic items, in which performers dress in traditional PIERROT costume.

Pin hinge   Hinge with a removable pin so that the two halves may be separated, used to provide a temporary connection between pieces of scenery.

Pipe   (American) BAR or BARREL.

Pit   Abbr. for ORCHESTRA PIT.

Area of AUDITORIUM seating in the centre of the lowest level.

Plant   Performer posing as a member of the audience, sometimes used by CONJURERS and related ACTS, but also occurring in plays such as *Our Town* by Thornton Wilder.

Plate   Small piece of thin ply used for reinforcing a joint in carpentry.

Plate spinning act   BALANCING ACT in which the performer performs various feats while balancing a spinning plate on the end of a thin rod, often seen in VARIETY or the CIRCUS.

Play   A dramatic work.

To act a role in a dramatic performance.

To perform at a specific venue, as in "to play the Hackney Empire".

Playbill   Theatre poster giving details of a performance.

A bold typeface with heavily elongated serifs frequently used on theatre posters.

Play broker   (American) Theatrical agent.

Play doctor   (or Play Fixer) One employed to re-write a play in an attempt to make it more successful, often after its OPENING NIGHT.

Player   Slightly antiquated term for an actor.

Playhouse   Theatre where plays are performed, especially those in London at the time of Shakespeare. (See GLOBE).

Play of ideas   Didactic play in which the playwright presents specific points of view to his audience, such as *An Enemy of the People* by Henrik Ibsen (1828-1906).

Play reader   One employed to read and assess plays submitted to a publisher or a theatre company.

Playscript   Written text of a play.

Play to the gallery   To aim one's performance at the least sophisticated members of the audience.

Play within a play   Play occurring as part of the dramatic action of a play. (eg. *Pyramus and Thisbe* in *A Midsummer Night's Dream*). (See SHOW WITHIN A SHOW).

Playwright   One who writes plays.

Plinge (Walter)   See WALTER PLINGE.

Plot   The storyline or action in a dramatic work.

A detailed list of lighting or effects CUES, or to prepare such a list.

Poached egg   A light filter made up by cutting the centre out of a frosted GEL so that it may be used with a coloured GEL to provide a diffused edge to a beam of light.

Poetic drama   A play written in a heightened language and rhythmic style, not necessarily in rhyme. Especially popular in the nineteenth century, modern examples include T. S. Eliot's *Murder in the Cathedral*, first performed in 1935.

Poetics   Aristotle's treatise on the structure and function of TRAGEDY. (See UNITIES).

Point shoes   Ballet dancers' shoes with a solid, blocked toe which supports the dancer's foot when balancing on the tip of the toe, or EN POINTE.

Political theatre   Drama dealing with political events or ideas, usually of a Marxist or left-wing nature. Bertolt Brecht (1898-1956) and Erwin Piscator (1893-1966) were two of its most celebrated exponents. Rarely commercially successful, contemporary political theatre is now usually confined to FRINGE productions or subsidised theatre companies.

Pollock's   A shop selling TOY THEATRES and printed sheets of scenery and characters founded by Benjamin Pollock (1856-1937) in Hoxton Street, London, now situated in Scala Street. (See PENNY PLAIN, TWOPENCE COLOURED.)

Popper   A press-stud fastener for clothing, especially useful on QUICK CHANGE COSTUMES.

Portal   Unit of semi-permanent masking consisting of WINGS and BORDER together. Two or three portals are sometimes used for complete MASKING. (In America the term is used to refer to the PROSCENIUM ARCH).

Practical   (Abbr. PRAC) Workable – applied to scenic elements such as doors or windows and to PROPS such as a lantern or a gramophone.

Premiere   The first ever performance of any theatrical piece.

Premièr Danseur   (French) Leading male dancer.

Première Danseuse   (French) Leading female dancer.

Preset   A special LIGHTING STATE necessary where HOUSE TABS are not used, which lights a SET in an appropriate manner before the performance begins.

To place PROPS or other items in position before they are required for use in a performance.

Preview   One or more special performances before the official OPENING NIGHT, usually with reduced admission prices.

Prima Ballerina   (Italian) Leading female dancer.

Prima Ballerina Assoluta (Italian) Title given by general acclaim to the most accomplished ballerina in a company.

Prima donna   Operatic LEADING LADY.

Priming   The first, preparatory coat when painting scenery, usually a mixture of SIZE and whiting.

Principal boy   Hero in PANTOMIME. Traditionally a transvestite role.

Principal girl   Heroine in PANTOMIME.

Producer   One who mounts a production, selecting the DIRECTOR, actors and leading technicians, and raising financial backing.

Production   A specific performance or RUN of performances of any theatrical work.

Production desk   Temporary desk with adjustable light, set in the centre of the AUDITORIUM, used by the DIRECTOR, LIGHTING DESIGNER etc. during technical preparations and DRESS REHEARSALS.

Production manager   (Abbr. P.M.) One with overall responsibility for the technical organisation of a production, including supervision of STAGE MANAGEMENT and TECHNICAL REHEARSALS, organising the SET UP and GET OUT and liaising with workshops, SCENE PAINTERS and WARDROBE departments.

Profile spot Spotlight giving a hard edged beam of light.

Profiling Plywood extension to the edge of a FLAT, cut to shape as designed.

Profit share Production in which participants work unpaid in return for a share of any profits, an arrangement often used in FRINGE productions. The actual profits are generally very little or nil.

Programme Booklet containing CAST LIST, list of scenes, various biographical and historical notes, and a good deal of advertising material, on sale before each performance.

Programme note Biographical or historical notes included in the PROGRAMME.

Any special item of information included in a PROGRAMME, such as an emergency cast change.

Project To perform so that voice and gestures are clearly conveyed to the rear of the AUDITORIUM.

To throw an image or silhouette onto a SET by means of a special LANTERN.

Projector A LANTERN designed to throw a painted or photographic image, or a silhouette, onto a SET.

(American) Floodlight.

Prologue An introductory scene or speech.

Actor performing a specially written introductory speech at the start of a play, as in Shakespeare's *Henry V.*

Promenade performance Performance with no audience seating. There are usually several different ACTING AREAS, the audience moving from one to the other to follow the action.

Prompt book (or PROMPT COPY) Master copy of the SCRIPT containing all actors' moves and technical CUES, used by a STAGE MANAGER to control the performance. (See BOOK).

Prompt corner   STAGE MANAGER'S control point at the side of the stage, traditionally STAGE LEFT.

Prompter   One who follows the text of a production in the SCRIPT and helps actors when they forget their lines.

Prompt side   See P.S.

Properties   (Abbr. PROPS) Furniture and other objects used by the actors during a performance. The term originated at The Theatre Royal, Drury Lane, when the great ACTOR MANAGER David Garrick (1717-1779) had every movable object labelled "Property of the Management."

Prop room   Room for storage or construction of PROPS.

Props   See PROPERTIES.

Prop table   Table set OFFSTAGE on which small PROPS are placed to be used by actors in performance.

Proscenium   (Abbr. PROS) The dividing wall between the stage and the AUDITORIUM, which contains the PROSCENIUM ARCH.

Proscenium arch   Architectural frame surrounding the opening in the proscenium wall, whether it is actually 'arched' or not, through which the performance is viewed.

Prose drama   Plays written in colloquial speech as opposed to POETIC or VERSE DRAMA.

Prosthesis   An artificial part of the body. The term usually refers to facial features, such as a false nose or sagging eyes, made from latex and blended into the skin with MAKE-UP after being fixed in place with SPIRIT GUM.

P.S.   Prompt Side. Stage left, from an actor's viewpoint when facing the audience.

Publicity manager/agent   One employed to promote a company, a production or an individual performer.

Pub theatre   Performance in a public house. Many pubs have a large room where a play may be performed to a small audience, and these provide a useful outlet for untried works. (See FRINGE).

Punch and Judy   Traditional glove puppet show, usually performed in a portable show-booth.

Purchase   See SINGLE PURCHASE or DOUBLE PURCHASE.

Push and pull   Special payments made to actors when they are required to move scenery or furniture during a performance, apart from when they are required to do so in character during the action of the play. Rates are established by EQUITY.

Pyrotechnics   (Abbr. PYROS) SPECIAL EFFECTS involving fireworks, such as explosions, flashes, or smoke.

Q

Quick change artist   A performer specialising in very rapid and contrasting changes in appearance.

Quick change costume   A costume made so that it may be removed as quickly as possible, often by means of a single fastening at the back. (See POPPER and VELCRO).

Quick change room   A small room at the side of the stage, often a makeshift structure built from un-needed FLATS, used by actors for costume changes when there is no time to return to the DRESSING ROOM.

R

RADA   The Royal Academy of Dramatic Art. A leading actors' training school, founded by Sir Herbert Beerbohm Tree in 1904 at His Majesty's Theatre. It has occupied its present premises in Gower Street, London since 1905.

Rag   See HOUSE CURTAIN.

Rail   Horizontal member in the timber framework of a FLAT.

Rain box   Shallow box or tray containing dried peas, to produce the sound of falling rain when rocked.

Rake Upward slope of the stage floor from front to back frequently found in older theatres, hence UPSTAGE and DOWNSTAGE.

Ramp ROSTRUM with a sloping top.

Razzle dazzle Glitter, style and energy combined to impress an audience and disguise a possible lack of genuine talent.

Reader See SCRIPT READER.

Read in To read an actor's lines from the script in his absence so that a rehearsal or, in an emergency, a performance may continue without him.

To help an actor to learn his lines by reading his CUES from the SCRIPT.

Reading See READ THROUGH and REHEARSED READING.

An actor's particular INTERPRETATION of the text.

Read through (or READING) The first rehearsal, at which the play is read aloud by the seated CAST.

Realism Form of staging using theatrical devices to produce the effect of reality. (cf. NATURALISM.)

Recast To select new actors for one or all of the roles in an existing production, often to replace actors leaving a long running show.

Receiving house Theatre which does not mount its own productions, but functions as a VENUE for touring shows and concerts.

Reflector Reflective surface at the back of a LANTERN which helps to direct and intensify the beam.

Régisseur Continental term for DIRECTORS.

Rehearsal Practice session for performers and/or technicians. A creative period when a DIRECTOR works with his COMPANY to establish the precise form the finished production will take.

Rehearsal props Substitute PROPS for use in REHEARSAL.

Rehearsal skirt Long skirt worn by actresses when rehearsing period plays to accustom themselves to wearing period costume.

Rehearsed reading Performance of a play in which no attempt is made at conventional staging, with actors reading their parts from the script. Often, a way of trying out new works at low cost.

Repertoire The schedule of performances. Two or more productions are rotated in the course of a SEASON.

Repertory (Abbr. REP) Production system employing a permanent group of actors, for plays of a limited RUN. There is normally one production in performance, another in REHEARSAL and several in varying degrees of planning at any one time.

Répétiteur One who coaches opera singers or dancers in their roles.

Resin box Tray of resin placed in the WINGS for dancers to apply to their shoes to prevent slipping.

Resting Out of work.

Restoration theatre Drama from the time of the Restoration of Charles II (1660). Many innovations in presentation occurred at this time: women first appeared on the public stage, footlights were introduced, and elaborate painted scenery was changed in full view of the audience. (See GROOVE SYSTEM.)

Return Narrow FLAT fixed at an angle to a wider one.

Returns Unwanted tickets returned to the BOX OFFICE for resale. (cf. BOX OFFICE RETURNS)

Reveal Narrow FLAT or piece of timber attached to the edge of an opening in a SET, such as a doorway or a window, to give the illusion of thickness to the surrounding wall.

Review CRITIC's published opinion of a production.

Revolve (or REVOLVING STAGE) Circular platform, built into the stage floor or set upon it, revolved by hand or winch, often electrically operated.

Revox   (Trade mark) Commonly used make of reel to reel tape recorder.

Revue   Form of light entertainment containing a mixture of musical and comedy items, popular from the late nineteenth century until the early 1960's.

Rhubarb   Word traditionally muttered by actors when required to produce the sound of background conversation.

Rhyming couplets   One of several forms of verse used mainly in classical drama, in which lines rhyme in pairs.

Rig   To set up lights for a performance.

The particular physical arrangement of lights for a performance.

To prepare a PROP or piece of scenery for a SPECIAL EFFECT.

Ringmaster   The circus's MASTER OF CEREMONIES, traditionally dressed in red coat and top hat.

Ripple effect   Special lighting effect which projects watery ripples onto scenery or the stage floor, by means of a revolving EFFECTS WHEEL or TUBULAR RIPPLE effect.

Riser   Vertical part of a step.

Road manager   One responsible for the practical organisation of a touring show, especially band shows of any kind.

Rockettes   (American) A famous female CHORUS LINE associated with Radio City Music Hall at Rockefeller Center in New York.

Role   The part played by a performer.

Role (in)   In the manner of the character portrayed.

Roller cloth   CLOTH attached to a long roller in such a way that it will wrap around the roller when not in use, generally used where there is a lack of FLYING SPACE.

Romantic comedy   Light entertaining play about people falling in love.

Romantic drama   Drama of the Romantic Revival of the late eighteenth and early nineteenth centuries. A DRAMATIST typical of this period was the German poet, Schiller (1759-1805).

Rough theatre Term coined by the director Peter Brook in his book *The Empty Space* (1968) to describe the degree of imperfection or 'roughness' present in all human activity, which he sees as an essential element in creativity.

Round A burst of applause.

Round off A burst of applause as an actor leaves the stage.

Rostrum Platform providing a raised area of stage floor. (Plural: Rostra – although rostrums is frequently heard).

Royal Box (The) A BOX, found in most WEST END THEATRES, usually at AUDITORIUM right, occupied by Royalty or distinguished visitors on formal visits, identified by the royal coat-of-arms above it.

Royal Court (The) A theatre in Sloane Square, London, whose productions were influential in the development of modern drama during the late 1950's and early 1960's. Its resident company, The English Stage Company, was founded to encourage new writing. One of its early successes was *Look Back In Anger* by John Osborne in 1956.

Royal Shakespeare Company (The) (Abbr. R.S.C.) A theatre company originally based at the Shakespeare Memorial Theatre in Stratford upon Avon to produce Shakespeare's plays, but now also playing in London and presenting plays by many other writers.

Royalty Percentage of profits or agreed sum of money paid to a writer, DIRECTOR, composer, or DESIGNER in return for the right to perform, reproduce or re-use his work.

Rug A wig.

Run Series of performances of the same production.

Several FLATS set in a straight line.

Abbr. for RUN THROUGH.

(As in "to run a flat") To hold a FLAT upright by one edge and move it smoothly across the stage.

Runners   Pair of TABS rigged to open at the centre.

Running time   Length of time a show or part of a show takes to perform.

Run through   REHEARSAL in which the complete production is rehearsed in the correct order.

S

Safety chain   Short length of chain with a spring hook at each end, used as a safety device when LANTERNS are hung from overhead bars.

Safety curtain   Fireproof shutter immediately behind the PROSCENIUM ARCH, lowered in the event of fire to completely seal off the stage area from the AUDITORIUM. The safety curtain must not be obstructed by scenery, and fire regulations require it to be lowered at every performance.

Samoiloff effect   Lighting technique used in SPECIAL EFFECTS, based upon the principle that a green object appears black under a red light and vice versa.

Sandbag   Canvas bag filled with sand, having a metal ring at the top, used as a weight for spare FLYING LINES.

Sandwich batten   Double wooden BATTEN supporting or weighting a CLOTH. The fabric is trapped between the two battens.

Sash cord   Strong, thin rope used for many purposes in connection with the FLYING SYSTEM (see BRAIL and BREAST), also for CLEAT LINES.

Saturation rig   LIGHTING RIG using every available LANTERN in every possible position.

Scatter   Spread of light outside the main beam.

Scene   One of the sections into which an ACT is sub-divided.

A stage SETTING.

Scène à faire   (French) The crucial scene to which preceding scenes build.

Scene dock   Storage area for scenery adjacent to the stage.

Scene painter   One who paints scenery of any kind, either built three-dimensional pieces or pictorial work on CLOTHS, enlarging the designer's MODELS and renderings to full size.

Scenery   SETTING in which a performance takes place, not necessarily representing 'location'.

Scene shifter   One who assists with scene changes during a performance.

Scenic gauze   Fine net with a hexagonal mesh used for special atmospheric effects. (See GAUZE).

Scissor move   Two actors crossing each other by moving across the stage at the same time in opposite directions. Generally thought to be undesirable.

Scissor stage   Method of changing scenery by means of TRUCKS pivoted at each side of the stage to be quickly and smoothly swung into position.

Score   Music for an OPERA or other musical show written down in musical notation. (cf. LIBRETTO).

Scottish Play (The)   Shakespeare's *Macbeth*. Euphemism used to avoid the bad luck supposed to be brought about by mentioning this play by name. (See Appendix B).

Scrim   To cover PROPS or scenery with glued fabric, either for protection or to provide a better surface for painting.

(American) GAUZE.

Script   See PLAYSCRIPT.

Script editor   One who prepares a SCRIPT for a particular production, cutting when required, sometimes transposing scenes or sections of dialogue, or even interpolating new sections.

Script reader   See PLAY READER.

Scumble Scene painting technique by which texture is applied by using short strokes in all directions with a nearly dry brush.

Seaside show A production presented at a seaside resort, primarily as entertainment for holiday-makers. (See PIERROT SHOW and CONCERT PARTY).

Season Series of productions spread over a period of pre-determined length.

Second cast Performers replacing all or part of the CAST of a show usually because the original performers have left for other work, or to allow them to rest during the RUN of a particularly strenuous show.

Segue To continue from one section to another without a break, originally a musical term but now applied generally, especially in LIGHTING and SOUND PLOTS.

Serge (black) Thick wool fabric with a black, non-reflective surface, used to cover MASKING FLATS and TORMENTORS.

Set (or SETTING) Complete scenery for whole or part of a production.

Group of three or four FLYING LINES used together to FLY one piece.

To place PROPS or scenery in position.

Set designer See DESIGNER.

Set dressing See DRESSING.

Set model Coloured scale model of a stage SETTING produced by the DESIGNER to demonstrate his design scheme.

Set of lines Group of FLYING LINES, usually three but sometimes five, spaced across the stage and operated together.

Set round Burst of applause in appreciation of the stage SETTING, usually occurring at CURTAIN UP.

Set speech Lengthy virtuoso soliloquy in a play, eg. Aston's speech in Pinter's *The Caretaker*, at the end of Act II.

Setting   See SET.

Setting line   Line on the stage floor parallel to the front edge of the stage from which measurements are taken when SETTING UP scenery.

Set up   See FIT UP.

   To prepare PROPS etc. for a performance.

Shadow play   Play performed with flat puppets behind a back-lit screen, the audience viewing the shadows thus created. Originating in China and Java, it was a popular form of entertainment in nineteenth century England.

Sharkstooth (gauze)   Fabric of rectangular mesh, suitable to be painted for special transparency effects. (See GAUZE).

Shin blasters/busters   LANTERNS set close to the floor at the sides of the stage, mainly in dance shows and BALLET.

'S' hook   Short length of wire bent into an 'S' shape, pushed through the canvas of a FLAT and used for hanging lightweight pictures etc.

Show   Any kind of performance.

Show business   The theatrical industry in general.

Showgirl   Female artiste, chosen for her good looks, who performs a mainly decorative function, adding glamour to a CABARET or REVUE type of entertainment.

Showman   Member of the STAGE CREW employed to work during performances only. (cf. DAYMAN).

Showmanship   Appreciation of what is theatrically effective and the ability to produce it.

Show must go on (The)   Phrase thought by the general public to encapsulate the traditional dedication of performers to their work. However, shows are frequently cancelled for a variety of reasons.

Show report   Written report made out by the COMPANY MANAGER after each performance, containing details of RUNNING TIMES, audience reaction and comments on any mistakes or unusual events. It is circulated to the PRODUCER, DIRECTOR, and THEATRE MANAGER.

Showstopper A particular item, usually in a musical show, which attracts so much applause that the performance is brought to a stand-still.

Show within a show Performance occurring as part of the dramatic action of a show. eg. *The Taming of the Shrew* in the musical *Kiss Me Kate*.

Shrink mirror Thin, flexible, reflective plastic, which may be stretched over a frame, then shrunk to remove wrinkles by applying heat, to make a convincing but lightweight mirror.

Shutter Adjustable device in front of a LANTERN to trim or alter the shape of a light beam.

Sight lines Imaginary lines, drawn on plans to indicate the limits of audience vision. They should always be carefully considered by the DESIGNER when planning his stage.

Silence An important element which can be remarkably effective in the theatre. The lengthy pauses in the plays of Harold Pinter (1930-) add dramatic strength to his dialogue. Before a circus artist performs an apparently difficult manoeuvre, he will often ask for complete silence to heighten its effectiveness.

Sill iron Strip of flat metal fastened across the bottom of an opening in a piece of scenery, such as a doorway, to lie flat on the floor and provide additional support.

Single purchase FLYING LINES without a system offering any MECHANICAL ADVANTAGE. (See DOUBLE PURCHASE).

Sitzprobe Seated music REHEARSAL for singers and musicians in OPERA.

Size Animal glue available in granular form to be dissolved in water and heated before use, frequently used in canvassing FLATS, and, mixed more thinly, for preparing canvas for painting (PRIMING) and fixing powder colours.

Skene   Permanent architectural background to the stage of an ancient Greek and Roman theatres. It housed actors' dressing rooms, and provided entrances to the stage.

Sketch   Short, usually humorous playlet performed as part of a VARIETY show.

Skip   Large travelling hamper for PROPS or COSTUMES.

Skit   Humorous parody.

Sky cloth   BACKCLOTH painted and lit to look like open sky.

Slap   Make-up.

Slapstick   Very broad, knockabout FARCE, often involving messy routines with materials such as water, flour and CUSTARD Pies. (See SLOSH).

Pair of thin wooden laths fastened together at one end, producing the noise of a loud slap when struck against an object. Traditionally carried by HARLEQUIN.

Slash   Stage curtain made of thin strips of a glittery material, hanging loose.

Slate   To damn with heavy criticism. The term usually refers to the professional theatre CRITICS' unfavourable reviews.

Sleeper   Play that is so boring it induces sleep.

Production that is expected eventually to attract larger audiences after a slow start.

Sleight of hand   See LÉGERDEMAIN.

Slice of life drama   Play in which the storyline is secondary to the effect of extreme realism in SETTING and style of acting.

Slips   The seats at the extreme ends of the upper tiers in a traditional 'horseshoe' shaped AUDITORIUM, usually with a severely restricted view of the stage.

Sloat   (Obsolete) Horizontal cut in the stage floor through which flat pieces of scenery, such as GROUNDROWS, may be raised from below.

Sloat box   Box positioned beneath the stage, containing a rolled, painted CLOTH to be raised through the SLOAT.

Slosh   (Or SPLOSH) Harmless, easily removed substitute for paste, cake-mix etc. used in SLAPSTICK scenes. Recipes are often jealously guarded by artists who specialise in SLAPSTICK. (See Appendix A).

Slosh cloth   Piece of STAGE CLOTH used to protect the stage floor during SLAPSTICK scenes.

Slot   Horizontal opening in the ceiling of the auditorium in which LANTERNS are hung.

Slow burn   Comic facial expression indicating seething anger. Its most celebrated exponent was Oliver Hardy of Laurel and Hardy.

S.M.   See STAGE MANAGER.

Smash hit   An exceptionally successful show.

Smoke gun   Machine for producing clouds of artificial smoke or mist. (cf. DRY ICE).

Smoke pellet   Small pellet which produces smoke when ignited, usually electrically. No flame is produced.

Snap line   (or CHALK LINE) Chalked length of thin cord stretched between two points and twanged to mark a straight line on scenery or the stage floor.

Snow bag   Canvas container for imitation snow, usually made from torn-up paper, which is rigged from the FLIES so that its contents may be gradually scattered onto the stage through holes cut in the canvas to simulate falling snow.

Social realism   Theatrical style in which social problems are addressed. Historically associated with the post-revolutionary theatre movement in Russia led by Anatoli Lunacharsky.

Sock it to them   To perform a song or dance routine in a particularly emphatic and energetic manner.

Soft masking   Stage MASKING made of DRAPES, not FLATS.

Softs   Stage draperies. (TABS, LEGS, BORDERS etc.)

Soft shoe (shuffle)   Gently rhythmic dance performed in shoes with soft leather soles, producing very little noise.

Soliloquy   Solo speech for an actor performed as part of a play. Hamlet's soliloquy beginning "To be, or not to be? . . ." is one of the best known soliloquies in all drama.

Solo   Vocal, instrumental or dance sequence for one performer.

Solo curtain/call   A CURTAIN CALL taken by one performer.

Son et lumière   (French) Sound and light. Performance with elaborate lighting and sound effects, but no visible performers, usually taking place in the open air at a location of architectural and historical interest.

Song sheet   Banner painted with the words of a song for community singing, nearly always used in PANTOMIME.

Scene in a PANTOMIME, in which the audience is encouraged to join in community singing, usually taking place before a FRONTCLOTH and forming the penultimate scene, allowing plenty of time to set elaborate scenery behind it for the WALK DOWN.

Soubrette   Actress specialising in young and coquettish roles, such as a pert maidservant.

Sound effect   Sound other than dialogue or music.

Sound level   Volume of a sound effect, established by the DIRECTOR before the TECHNICAL REHEARSAL.

Sound plot   List of all sound effects required in a performance, together with notes of SOUND LEVELS and CUES that precipitate them.

Sparge pipe   The SAFETY CURTAIN's drencher pipe, used only in emergency. (See SPRINKLER).

Sparks   See ELECTRICS.

Spatter   Scene painting technique by which paint is flicked from a brush to achieve a fine speckled texture.

Spear carrier   An EXTRA, especially one engaged solely to add authenticity to a historical scene as a guard or attendant. Often used as a derogatory term for an unsuccessful actor.

Special   LANTERN positioned for one specific effect.

Special effects   Term embracing any unusual or specific effect from a complete TRANSFORMATION SCENE to the pop of a champagne cork.

Speciality act   VARIETY act in which the performer displays skill in a particular field such as juggling or playing an instrument, often inserted into a MUSICAL SHOW or PANTOMIME.

Speech   Extended solo passage in a play.

Spike   Nail. (Both as a noun and a transitive verb).

Spill   Unwanted light spreading from a LANTERN.

Spirit gum   Adhesive for sticking hair-pieces etc. to the face.

Split week   A week in which the production is changed on a Thursday instead of, as is more usual, at the weekend.

Splosh   See SLOSH.

Spot   A SPOTLIGHT.

Spot bar   Counterweighted BAR suspended above the stage from which LANTERNS are hung.

Spotlight   LANTERN with a focusable beam.

The most commonly used CASTING DIRECTORY, containing photographs of actors available for work.

Spot line   A single line rigged from the GRID, used for hanging chandeliers etc.

Spring hook   Metal hook closed with a metal bar on a spring, similar to that found on a dog leash.

S.R.O.   (American) Standing Room Only. A full HOUSE.

Stage   A performing space.

To mount a production.

Stage (The)   A weekly newspaper aimed at the theatrical profession. Established in 1880.

Stage adaptation   Version of a novel re-written to be performed in the theatre.

Stage box   One of the auditorium BOXes nearest to the stage.

Stage brace   Adjustable support for scenery, used in conjunction with a STAGE WEIGHT or STAGE SCREW.

Stage business   See BUSINESS.

Stage cloth   Sheet of painted canvas covering the stage floor.

Stagecraft   Technical skills, employed by stage technicians, performers, directors and writers.

Stage crew   Team of STAGEHANDs working on the preparation or running of a show. Generally applied to those engaged in heavier work, such as scene shifting.

Stage directions   Notes in the script suggesting actions or MOVEs to be performed by actors.

Stage director   One in overall charge of stage staff and activities taking place on the stage.

Stage door   Access to BACKSTAGE areas from outside the theatre.

Stage door Johnny   Edwardian term applied to a man, usually wealthy and/or upper class, who tries to gain admittance at the STAGE DOOR to make assignations with the attractive female members of the company.

Stage doorman   (or STAGE DOOR KEEPER) One employed to check all those entering by the STAGE DOOR, relay messages to the actors and BACKSTAGE staff, and to issue and collect DRESSING ROOM keys.

Stage fright   Incapacitating nervousness when required to appear on stage.

Stagehand   Member of the STAGE CREW.

Stagehouse   That part of the theatre building containing the stage as opposed to the AUDITORIUM.

Stage left　Left-hand side of the stage from the actor's point of view. Traditionally, this is the side from which evil characters enter in a PANTOMIME.

Stageman　(American) STAGEHAND.

Stage management　All those responsible for organising and running technical aspects of rehearsals and performances.

Stage manager　(Abbr. S.M.) One in overall charge of the stage during rehearsals and performances.

Stage name　The name by which a performer is known professionally. EQUITY will not allow two members to work under the same name, so new members are sometimes forced to adopt a name other than their own.

Stage plan　(or GROUND PLAN) A scale plan of the stage showing positions of scenery and furniture.

Stager　(American) Archaic term for an actor.

Stage right　Right-hand side of the stage from the actor's point of view.

Stagery　(American) STAGECRAFT.

Stage school　School where children can receive education at the same time as being trained for the theatre.

Training school for actors and theatre technicians of all ages.

Stage screw　Screw with a large metal loop, screwed into the stage floor by hand to secure the foot of a STAGE BRACE.

Stage set　See SET.

Stage-struck　Obsessed with ambition to perform in theatre.

Stage weight　(or BRACE WEIGHT) Heavy metal weight used to secure the foot of a STAGE BRACE.

Stage whisper　Actor's technique of projecting a 'whispered' line so that the words may be clearly heard by the audience.

Stagey   Obviously artificial.

Stagger through   An early attempt at a RUN THROUGH.

Stalls   Main AUDITORIUM seating at ground level.

Stand-up comic   COMEDIAN who performs solo, without FEED or STRAIGHTMAN, popular in VARIETY and Working Men's Clubs.

Star system   Commercial promotion of shows by the fame of the leading performer(s) rather than any other qualities.

Star trap   Small hexagonal or octagonal trapdoor made by hinging six or eight triangles around the perimeter. Machinery beneath the stage permits a performer to make a sudden appearance by shooting upwards through the stage floor. Traditionally used by demons etc. in PANTOMIME and, therefore, often situated DOWNSTAGE left. (See STAGE LEFT)

Stealing one's thunder   See THUNDER SHEET.

Stile   Vertical member of the timber framework of a FLAT.

Stock company   Nineteenth century term applied to group of actors performing a REPERTOIRE of plays. Actors generally specialised in a certain type of role, such as villain, old man, or young lover. It is a somewhat derogatory term implying a rather crude acting style.

Stooge   See FEED.

Straight man   Actor performing as a foil to a COMIC rather than raising laughs himself.

Straight play   Play without music.

Straight theatre   Dramatic, as distinct from musical theatre or VARIETY.

Street theatre   Informal performances in the street, played to passers-by. A collection is usually taken.

Strike   To remove a SETTING or a PROP from the stage during a performance.

To dismantle and remove a production from the theatre at the end of a RUN.

Stripper   Exponent of STRIPTEASE.

Stripping   Disguising a join between two FLATS by gluing a strip of muslin or thin CANVAS over it and painting to match.

Striptease   Entertainment in which the performer removes successive items of clothing in a deliberate attempt at sexual stimulation. Popular in BURLESQUE.

Strobe   Device emitting a series of very bright flashes of light at an adjustable speed. It has the effect of apparently reducing movement to a series of rapid jerks.

Strolling players   Itinerant groups of professional actors, especially of the seventeenth century, travelling from town to town and performing wherever an audience could be raised.

Strut one's stuff   To display one's talent before an audience.

Studio theatre   Informal performing space, often attached to larger theatres, used for small-scale or experimental works. The ACTING AREA and seating may be varied as required.

Sugar glass   Imitation glass made from sugar solution, used to make window panes, bottles and glasses, which may then be harmlessly broken during a performance. (See APPENDIX A)

Summerstock   American provincial theatre companies playing during the summer months.

Super   (Abbr. for Supernumerary). One who appears in a performance but has no lines of dialogue. (See EXTRA).

Supertrooper   A powerful carbon-arc FOLLOW SPOT.

Surprise pink   Lighting GEL of a mauve-pink colour, giving a particularly glamourous and flattering effect by intensifying both warm and cold colours.

Surtitles   English translation of the words sung or spoken in a foreign language production, usually OPERA, projected above the PROSCENIUM ARCH.

Swag   Curtain rigged to be raised in the form of a curved drape by means of a line passing through rings sewn to the back.

Switchboard   Stage lighting control board.

Swivel arm   Short pivoted BAR used for hanging LEGS from the FLIES so that the angle in relation to the PROSCENIUM may be easily adjusted.

Synopsis   Outline of the plot of a play or musical show, usually submitted to a PRODUCER before the final script is written.

T

Tableau   (French: Picture). Continental equivalent of SCENE, used in English to refer to the stage "picture" obtained by a particular scenic effect and/or the grouping of performers.

Tableau vivant   (French: Living picture). Representation of a well known picture or piece of statuary by a performer or performers in costume, who remain motionless and silent.

Tabs   (Abbr. for tableau curtains) Pair of stage curtains, sometimes rigged to part horizontally, sometimes FLOWN.

Tab track   Heavy duty curtain track on which TABS are FLOWN so that they may be opened or closed horizontally.

Tab warmers   LANTERNS set specially to light the HOUSE TABS before a performance, during the INTERVAL or in a scene break.

Take   A glance thrown by an actor towards an object or another actor in such a way that it is clearly seen by the audience. (See DOUBLE TAKE)

Take off   To impersonate.

Talent contest/show　Show in which unknown amateur performers compete with each other in the hope of being "discovered". The winner is usually chosen by audience acclaim.

Talent scout　One employed to seek out unknown talented performers.

Tallescope　Expendable vertical ladder with wheeled support, especially useful for adjusting high hanging LANTERNS.

Tannoy　BACKSTAGE sound relay system. (cf. P.A.)

Tap dance　(Abbr. TAP) Lively dance style with rapid rhythmic tapping of the feet.

Tap shoes　Dance shoes with metal plates attached to the soles at the toes and/or heels.

Teaser　Black BORDER hung between the TORMENTORS provide top MASKING.

(American) TORMENTOR.

Technical director　One with overall responsibility for all technical aspects of the stage.

Technical rehearsal　(Abbr. TECH) Rehearsal primarily intended for the technical aspects of a production, such as scene changes, sound effects and lighting, rather than the actors' performances.

Theatre　Building in which performances of any kind take place.

Place of entertainment.

The abstract relationship between performer(s) and audience.

Theatre chaplain　Member of the local clergy attached to a theatre, often a frequent BACKSTAGE visitor.

Theatre-in-the-round　Performance in which the ACTING AREA is completely surround by audience.

Theatre of cruelty　Term coined by Antoine Artaud (1896-1948) to describe a sensual, rather than intellectual, style of theatre, not dependent upon the spoken word.

Theatre of the absurd   Theatrical movement of the 1950's which produced plays of a surrealist nature by writers such as Samuel Beckett and Eugene Ionesco.

Theatre Workshop   Theatre company established in 1953 at The Theatre Royal, Stratford, East London, by Joan Littlewood. The company played an important part in the development of political theatre in Britain.

Theban Plays (The)   *Oedipus the King, Antigone* and *Oedipus at Colonus*. Three plays by the Greek dramatist Sophocles (496-406 B.C.) telling the story of Oedipus.

Thespian   Antiquated term for an actor, from Thespis of Icaria, an ancient Greek poet generally considered to be the founder of drama.

Three-hander   Play for three performers.

Thriller   Play with a sensational plot designed to entertain by the excitement it produces.

Throat mike   Small radio microphone worn unobtrusively on a performer's COSTUME near the throat. (See CONTACT MIKE)

Throw   Length of a beam of light.

Throw a line   To throw a CLEAT LINE over the CLEAT HOOK at the top of a FLAT. Experienced STAGE HANDs take pride in performing this action skilfully.

To PROMPT.

Throw-away line   A line of dialogue deliberately delivered with little PROJECTion.

Throw line   See CLEAT LINE.

Thrust stage   Stage which juts forwards into the audience.

Thunder run   Long wooden chute, now obsolete, situated above the stage, down which cannon balls were rolled to give the effect of thunder.

Thunder sheet   Large sheet of metal, usually hung in the FLY GALLERY, which, when shaken by one corner, produces a clap of thunder. It was first used during the seventeenth century in a play by John Dennis, and considered a great improvement on the old THUNDER RUN. Later, when he heard the thunder sheet used by a rival, he remarked "Sir, you have stolen my thunder!" This expression is still used to describe an actor stealing applause from another.

Ticket tout   'Black marketeer' who acquires tickets for popular shows and re-sells them at inflated prices.

T.I.E.   Theatre In Education. Theatre company performing specifically to school children, usually in school venues.

Tie off   To fasten a rope or LINE securely to a CLEAT.

Tights   A close fitting garment covering the body from the waist down, frequently including the feet, usually made from cotton jersey or other stretch fabric.

Time play   One of several plays by J. B. Priestley, such as *Time and the Conways*, which manipulate time as a dramatic device.

Timing   The variations in the speed at which a scene is played, or the precise moment that a line of dialogue or a specific effect is performed to gain the best dramatic or humorous impact. A crucial element in any performance.

Toby   (or DOG TOBY) A small live dog which traditionally takes part in a PUNCH AND JUDY show.

Toggle   Short length of timber, tapered at each end, used in the construction of FLATS to attach the centre rail STILES.

Toi toi toi   To wish "good luck" on the Continent. It is a stylised form of spitting over the shoulder for luck. (See BREAK A LEG)

Top (The)   Start of a scene or Act, as in "Take it from the top" meaning "start at the beginning of the scene."

Top and tail   Method of speeding up a TECHNICAL REHEARSAL by omitting dialogue from lengthy speeches, but retaining the last lines so that the correct CUES are given.

Top hat   Black metal cylinder designed to fit in front of a LANTERN to reduce SCATTER.

Top of the bill   The leading act in a VARIETY show, therefore printed at the top of the posters.

Torch song   Mournful type of song, popular in nightclubs of the 1930's, usually performed by a female singer, expressing the pain of love.

Tormentor   Plain black MASKING FLAT set at either side of the stage, immediately UPSTAGE of the PROSCENIUM.

Total theatre   An elaborately flexible theatre, extremely radical in design, proposed by the German architect Walter Gropius in 1926. It was never built.

Toupee tape   Double sided adhesive tape for fixing wigs in place.

Touring company   A theatre company which travels from place to place presenting a show or REPERTOIRE of shows for a limited period at each VENUE.

Toy theatre   A popular toy throughout all ages. (See POLLOCKS)

Track   Heavy duty curtain track for hanging TABS.

Tragedy   Play relating a sad or tragic story in an elevated poetic style. *Oedipus the King* by Sophocles (496-406 B.C.) is typical of classical Greek tragedy. *King Lear* by Shakespeare (1564-1616) is an Elizabethan example.

Tragic carpet   Green baize floor covering, in use from the seventeenth to the nineteenth centuries, to protect the COSTUMES of actors required to "die" on stage.

Transfer   To move a provincial show into a London theatre, or from London to a New York theatre or vice versa.

Transformation flat   Special FLAT, often used in the TRANSFORMATION SCENE of traditional PANTOMIME, with a painted CANVAS flap attached to the face which may be dropped in order to "magically" change its appearance.

Transformation piece   Piece of false hair used in combination with the actor's own hair to add extra length or fullness.

Transformation scene   PANTOMIME effect in which the scene "magically" changes to another by the use of special techniques such as GAUZES and TRANSFORMATION FLATS.

Transparency   CLOTH or part of a cloth painted in dyes or thinned paint and lit from behind.

Trap   Section of the stage floor which can be removed to form an opening.

Trap room   Area underneath the stage to which the TRAPS give access.

Traveller   (or TRAVERSE CURTAIN or WIPE) A curtain, often with a painted design, which may only be drawn across the stage from one side instead of opening in the centre.

Travelling players   Troupes of itinerant professional actors.

Traverse curtain   See TRAVELLER.

Traverse stage   A long stage with the audience seated at either side.

Treads   Steps.

The flat, horizontal part of a step.

Tread the boards   To ACT on stage.

Tree border   (or LEAF BORDER) Canvas BORDER cut and painted to suggest foliage, often used to complete an exterior scene.

Tripe   Lengths of electric cable in the FLIES connecting the LIGHTING BARS to the outlets at the side of the stage.

Trouper   An indefatigable performer, especially in VARIETY.

Truck   (or BOAT TRUCK) Platform on castors carrying all or part of a SET, so that it may be easily moved into its position ONSTAGE.

Truss Strong metal framework, usually a temporary structure, erected across the ACTING AREA or AUDITORIUM to support LANTERNS etc.

Tubular ripple Lighting device which projects the effect of water ripples by passing light through a revolving cylinder with irregular wavy slits cut into the sides.

Tumble To FLY a CLOTH on two SETS OF LINES by attaching a second set to the bottom of the CLOTH, thus causing it to double in half when FLOWN. Useful where there is insufficient FLYING SPACE.

Tumbler CLOTH rigged to TUMBLE.

Turfer A cable tensioning device.

Turn A VARIETY act.

Tutu Costume worn by BALLERINAS with a very short, stiff, spreading skirt, so that the line of legs and body may be seen to best effect.

Two-hander Play for two performers.

Type casting Selecting actors for roles by physical appearance and personality, or their established familiarity in certain roles, rather than acting ability.

U

Über-marionette (German: Super-puppet). Term coined by the DESIGNER Edward Gordon Craig (1872-1966) to describe his ideal actor, performing in a strongly stylised manner, with no emotional involvement.

Underplay To act in an unexaggerated way, with few external signs of emotion. Paradoxically, when skilfully done, underplaying can be very dramatically effective.

Understudy One who learns and rehearses a part being played by another actor so that he may take over the role in an emergency.

Unities   The Unities of Time, Place and Action were developed from Aristotle's theories of dramatic construction and, in part, laid down in his essays *On the Art of Poetry,* (*The Poetics*). They require the action of a TRAGEDY (drama) to take place within twenty four hours (Time), with no change of location (Place), and with one single plot (Action).

Upstage   Area of the stage furthest from the audience.

> (Verb – "to upstage") A technique sometimes unfairly employed by an actor to place himself in a more favourable position than his fellows by moving slightly towards the back of the stage, thus forcing any other actors playing with him to turn away from the audience in order to maintain contact.

U.V.   (or BLACK LIGHT) Ultra Violet light. Normally invisible light which causes special pigments to fluoresce in a BLACKOUT.

V

Vac-formed   Moulded from sheet plastic by a vacuum process. A technique used to reproduce decorative features on scenery, PROPS etc.

Vandyke crystals   Strong brown dye in the form of water soluble crystals, used by SCENE PAINTERS for BREAKING DOWN, GRAINING etc.

Variable beam spotlight   PROFILE SPOT with two lenses to adjust the beam in width, or from a hard to a soft edge.

Variation   Solo dance, part of a sequence of dances in BALLET.

Variety   Popular form of entertainment consisting of assorted items – musical, comic, or acrobatic, no longer as popular as it was before the advent of television.

Vaudeville   American VARIETY.

Vehicle Production mounted to display the talents of a specific performer, or to express a specific point of view.

Velcro Double tape with a short stiff pile that will adhere firmly to itself but may be easily pulled apart, useful as a fastening on a QUICK CHANGE COSTUME.

Velour Heavy, short-piled fabric which hangs well and looks luxurious when lit, frequently used for stage curtains.

Venue Any location where a performance may take place.

Verse drama Play written in verse such as *The Cocktail Party* by T. S. Eliot (1888-1939).

Voice coach One employed to train a performer's speaking voice.

Vomitory (Abbr. VOM) Special access to the stage from the AUDITORIUM, usually by means of a passage beneath the seating, often used in THEATRE IN THE ROUND.

W

Walk To move about the stage under the direction of the LIGHTING DESIGNER so that he can check that actors are properly lit in all positions. A task usually performed by a member of the STAGE MANAGEMENT when light LEVELS are being set.

Walk down Final scene of a PANTOMIME or REVUE in which all artists taking part acknowledge applause, usually descending a decorative flight of steps.

Walking gentleman/lady Victorian term for an actor playing a small supporting role.

Walk-on part A role with no dialogue.

Walk up (As in "to walk up a flat") To raise a large FLAT from the floor by wedging the bottom of it against a wall, or someone's foot, then lifting it to a vertical position by moving up the STILES hand over hand.

Walter Plinge A fictitious name sometimes inserted into the CAST LIST when, for any reason, it is undesirable to give the name of the actor playing a part.

Wardrobe General name for the COSTUME department, its staff, and the premises they occupy.

Wardrobe mistress/supervisor One in overall charge of the COSTUME department.

Warm up A period of active preparation for performers before appearing on stage or rehearsing, consisting of vocal and/or physical exercises.

Water dimmer Antiquated method of dimming stage lights using water filled cylinders.

Water Rats (The Grand Order of) Association of MUSIC-HALL and VARIETY performers. Since its formation in 1889 it has raised large sums for charity and needy artists.

Ways Electrical channels in the control system.

Web and tape Length of webbing with twin tapes at regular intervals, stitched along the top edge of a DRAPE or CLOTH to attach it to a BATTEN.

Weekly rep REPERTORY in which a new production is presented each week, now generally obsolete.

Well made play A technically well constructed work, regardless of artistic merit.

West end theatre Those (mostly commercial) theatres centred upon Shaftesbury Avenue in London.

Wet white Liquid body MAKE-UP, not necessarily white.

Whitehall farce One of a series of popular farces which were performed at the Whitehall Theatre in London during the late 1940's and 50's. Its most celebrated leading man was Brian Rix, appearing in such plays as *Reluctant Heroes* and *Dry Rot*.

Whodunnit   Play in which the audience is encouraged to try to guess who has perpetrated a crime or series of crimes. A typical example is *The Mousetrap*, the long running play by Agatha Christie.

Wiggle pins   Corrugated fasteners. 'Nails' made from a short section of corrugated metal.

Winch   Winding mechanism for operating TABS or moving TRUCKS and REVOLVES, either motorised or hand-operated.

Wind machine   Wooden drum with slats around the sides, revolved against a strip of taut CANVAS to produce the sound of whistling wind.

Wing flats   FLATS used as WINGS, sometimes with PROFILING on the leading edge, and often BOOKED. (BOOK WINGS)

Wings   Areas at the sides of the stage beyond the scenery.

Vertical pieces of scenery or fabric (LEGS) used to mask the areas at the sides of the stage.

Wipe   See TRAVELLER.

Women's Institute drama   Plays such as those performed by Women's Institutes and similar organisations, generally consisting of a number of parts for women and few, if any, male roles.

Word of mouth   Publicity in the form of informal personal recommendation by those who have already seen a production.

Workers   (or WORKING LIGHTS) Lights used to illuminate the stage for REHEARSALS or technical work.

Working drawings   Scale drawings of scenery or PROPS used for construction.

Working lights   See WORKERS.

Workshop   Premises set aside for constructing and painting scenery and PROPS.

A firm contracted to construct and/or paint scenery and PROPS.

X Y Z

Xylophonist   A once popular VARIETY act.

Yawn   A boring production.

"Yes?" Spoken by actors in rehearsal when requesting a PROMPT.

Yiddish drama   Plays on Jewish themes performed in Yiddish. The Yiddish theatre movement originated among Russian and German Jews in the late eighteenth century.

York Mystery Cycle   A series of medieval MYSTERY PLAYS still performed in York.

Youth theatre   Performances aimed at, and created by, young people.

Zanni   Servant characters of the COMMEDIA DELL'ARTE. In Elizabethan times it was used as a derogatory term for an inept performer.

Zarzuela   Spanish play with music, usually light in character. The name derives from the royal shooting-lodge near Madrid where such entertainments took place during the reign of Philip IV.

Ziegfeld follies   See FOLLIES.

APPENDICES

APPENDIX A

Recipe for *SLOSH*:

Finely grate a stick of shaving soap into a bucket. (*Erasmic* refills work well and do not smell too much).

Mix in just enough water to make a stiff 'goo'. Use a powerful electric drill on slow speed with an industrial beater or piece of bent metal to whip up the mixture, adding water as required. Add two tablespoonsful of cornflour in water to the mixture and remix at high speed.

Colour with *Boots* food colouring for least staining.

Recipe for *SUGAR GLASS*:

Prepare a supersaturated solution of sugar and water (that is, a solution with as much sugar absorbed by the water as possible) and heat to about 260 degrees Fahrenheit. Pour onto a smooth surface in a thin layer. The solution will harden into a clear transparent solid that may be used as a glass substitute when it is desired to break windows on stage. It has the disadvantage of a low melting point that may cause the sugar glass to soften under stage lighting.

Recipe for *STAGE BLOOD*:

Mix *Gordon Moore's Cosmetic Toothpaste* with glycerine.

This 'blood' is non-toxic, palatable and generally non-staining, but if 'non-staining' is crucial, test on fabric first.

The above recipes are from information cards issued by the A.B.T.T.

Appendix B

Common Theatrical Superstitions

Considered unlucky:

Quoting, or even mentioning, *Macbeth*. (The antidote is to apologise to the STAGE MANAGER).

Whistling in the dressing room. (The antidote is to step outside and turn round three times).

A green SET.

A green COSTUME.

Real flowers used on stage.

A real Bible used on stage.

Speaking the last RHYMING COUPLET of a PANTOMIME before the FIRST NIGHT.

Rehearsing the CURTAIN CALL before the DRESS REHEARSAL.

Wishing an actor "good luck" before a performance. (See BREAK A LEG and TOI TOI TOI).

Considered lucky:

Being pricked by a pin at a COSTUME FITTING. (Especially if some blood gets on the costume).

Finding a length of thread adhering to a COSTUME. (It means that a new contract is about to be offered, the lenght of the thread indicating the length of the contract).

Oberon Books Limited, 8 Richardson Mews, London W1P 5DF
Tel: 071-383 5569.

Please send _____ copies of *The Oberon Glossary of Theatrical Terms* at £4.95 per copy (subject to alteration). I enclose £ _____ plus 50 pence per copy for postage and packing (maximum £2.50).

Name: _____

Address: _____

_____

Telephone: _____